CW01373904

Saudi Arabia

Saudi Arabia

Shirley Kay
DRAWINGS BY MALIN BASIL

Namara
Publications

First published by Namara Publications Limited 1979
Namara House
45/46 Poland Street, London W1

Set in Monotype Horley Old Style
by Clerkenwell Graphics,
London E1

Designed by Mike Jarvis

ISBN 0 7043 2223 4

Made and printed in Great Britain by
The Garden City Press Limited
Letchworth, Hertfordshire SG6 1JS

CONTENTS

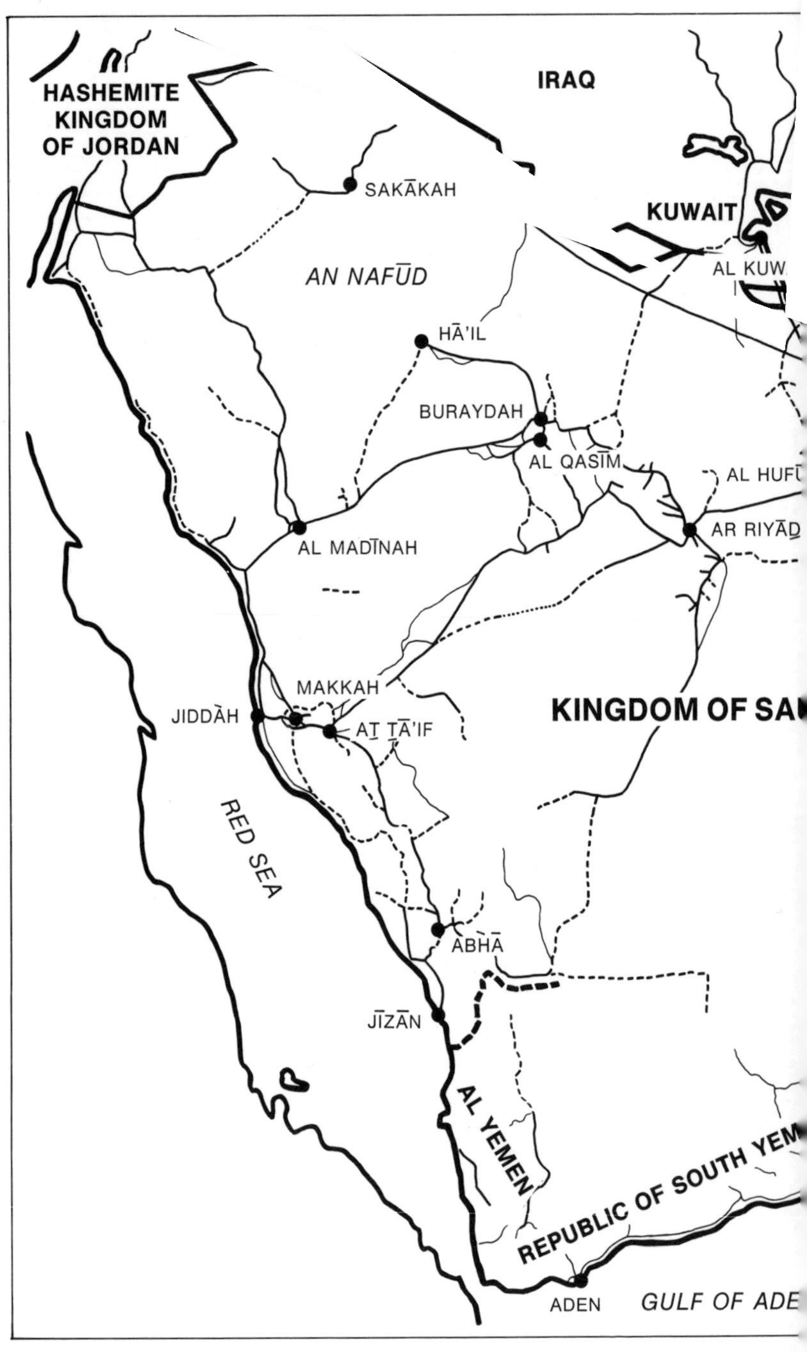

HASHEMITE KINGDOM OF JORDAN
IRAQ
SAKĀKAH
KUWAIT
AN NAFŪD
HĀ'IL
BURAYDAH
AL QASĪM
AL MADĪNAH
MAKKAH
JIDDĀH
AṮ TĀ'IF
KINGDOM OF SA
RED SEA
ABHĀ
JĪZĀN
AL YEMEN
REPUBLIC OF SOUTH YEM
ADEN
GULF OF ADE

IRAN
AHRAIN
ARABIAN GULF
QATAR
DUBAI
ABU DHABI
GULF OF OMAN
MASQAT
UNITED ARAB EMIRATES
ABIA
AR RUB' AL KHĀLĪ
SULTANATE OF OMAN
ARABIAN SEA
MUKALLĀ
International boundary
Major road – surfaced
Major road – under construction
Other roads – unpaved
Road – under design

Acknowledgements

The preparation of the text and illustrations for this book was facilitated in many ways by various friends and institutions. We wish to express our thanks to the Ministry of Information of the Kingdom of Saudi Arabia for their valuable help and advice throughout the project; to SIYANCO, Saudi Maintenance Company Ltd, for supplying cars and drivers and other logistic support during our travels throughout the Kingdom; and finally to all those friends who smoothed our travels by offering us their hospitality.

1
Riyadh and the Nejd

From the tawny sand and gravel plain of the Nejd rises the great desert city of Riyadh, capital of Saudi Arabia. Although its name, ar-Riyadh, means 'gardens' and is not deceptive, for the town was originally built around the luxuriant palm gardens of the Wadi Hanifa, it is for all that a pure desert city. Its air is the dry, clear air of the desert, invigorating in winter, hot as an oven in summer but not exhausting like the humid atmosphere of the coastal plains to east and west. At night the temperature drops to the cool of a desert night.

The city has the colour of the desert from which it has sprung: its beige tones range from white through to brown with the warm tawny hues of the mud buildings predominating in the old town. Beyond the end of the new dual carriageways with their high metal lamp-posts the desert colours show again, deep tones in the early morning, glaring white and yellow at noon, glowing golden brown at eventide.

Within this desert setting Riyadh is an almost entirely modern city, grown from an estimated population of 25,000 in 1912 when an Englishman, Leachman, first visited 'the great capital of Nejd', to an extensive town of over three-quarters of a million inhabitants today. Many of the wide main streets of modern Riyadh have dual carriageways lined with well-developed palm trees along the central reservations. Its skyline is marked by high-rise office and apartment blocks and the elegant new Ministry buildings in well-planted gardens along the Airport Road.

A few of the modern buildings have come to be known as special landmarks of Riyadh. Most characteristic perhaps, and most frequently photographed, is the elegant, flaring, black-and-white-striped water tower set dramatically in a wide, well-gardened square in the Murabba district, its ultra-modern lines contrasting with the squat mud walls of old palaces fronting the square. It is appropriate

THE RIYADH WATER TOWER

that the 60-metre-high water tower should have become almost the symbol of the city, for life in Riyadh depends entirely on the management of deep underground water resources. Its old wells are some of the deepest in use in the world; the pressure in its water network is maintained thanks to modern engineering such as the high water tower.

On the northern outskirts of the city are a series of buildings and developments which are also earning world renown. First of these perhaps is the King Faisal Specialist Hospital, providing highly sophisticated medical care for people who, two generations ago, often did not even have aspirins. Entering the King Faisal Hospital is like coming into an expensive modern hotel: floors and walls are carpeted, mosaics and murals decorate the corridors, the atmosphere is quiet and cool, there is no 'hospital' smell or atmosphere at all. The wards too are reminiscent of hotel rooms, attractively furnished, equipped with television, curtains and lights controlled by switches from the bed.

Medical and nursing staff and specialists have been brought from all over the world to provide the hospital with the highest skills. Any Saudi can become a patient there if his illness is such that he is referred from another hospital. If he cannot afford to pay for himself, the state will foot the bill.

Another striking building which dates from the reign of the late King Faisal is the Conference Hall, built in the same complex as the Intercontinental Hotel. These buildings are set quietly into a gentle, well-gardened hillside on the edge of the desert. The Hall provides extensive and supremely comfortable conference facilities including a main lecture hall to seat 1400, with suede armchairs for delegation leaders and behind the stage a massive gold and malachite Saudi coat of arms. The hotel, with its layers of internal balconies looking down onto the main reception area, is linked to the Conference Hall by dining rooms including a banqueting hall for 1000 people which can be approached from both Hall and Hotel, making maximum use of the catering facilities.

Possibly more spectacular then either of these functional buildings will be the Olympic Sports City, currently under construction on a high bluff above the Wadi Hanifa and offering a panoramic view over the city below. This huge sports complex, covering $5\frac{1}{4}$ square kilometres, is a symbol of the Saudis' determination to rise above their environment, to play world-class sport in temperatures which in summer can soar to 120°F. Pride of the complex is to be the great football stadium, to seat 80,000 spectators, and to set a seal on the national passion for this sport above all others.

A quieter use of the city's open spaces is in the small gardens which have been developed here and there to provide an oasis of green among the asphalt. Grander parks are also under construction: in the planning department is a large working model of an extensive safari park to be built outside the town. The lights flash on, the models move; they show a Disneyland, a wild animal reserve, a cultural area, and a mosque to hold 1000 worshippers.

South-east of the city, and also on the fringe of the desert, lie the industrial areas ranging from car workshops and small back-street mechanics to the modern industrial estate and – further out still – the petrol refinery. A number of factories of varying sizes have been built on the industrial estate where the government provides land and amenities at a nominal rent. Private-sector industrial development is encouraged by the state as a corner-stone of the kingdom's future economy. The industrial estates of Riyadh, Jeddah and Damman are producing furniture and spring mattresses, paper products, pipes, foam plastic, air conditioners

DOORWAY IN HAIL

and desert coolers, paints, aluminium door and window frames, barrels, space heaters and so forth.

The districts which give the city its unique character are not, however, these modern ones but rather the quiet shady alleys of the older parts of the town with their fine mud houses and palaces, reminders of a bygone age. These old buildings of mud and chopped straw are faced with a smooth mud finish, often decorated with a row of dog-tooth triangles a little below the roof line. The latter is usually ornamented with lines of small stepped pyramids known as crowstep. Both forms of decoration are of ancient origin, known from the buildings and relief pictures of Babylon and ancient Assyria. The crowstep style reached its peak in the Nabataean rock-cut tombs of Petra and Medain Salih, and has remained popular in central and south-west Arabia ever since.

The little lanes between these mud buildings sometimes still have sand underfoot, deadening the sound of footfalls and absorbing rather than reflecting back the heat. Above one's head rows of

A MOSQUE IN THE NEJD

wooden gutters project from the walls just below the roof line, to carry off the winter rainfall from the flat roofs.

Many of these buildings were in fact constructed in the twentieth century, though to a time-honoured plan. The Murabba Palace, home of the kingdom's great founder, King Abd al Aziz ibn Saud, was built in the 1930s. Its wide courtyards, surrounded by colonnades at ground and first-floor level, might have graced an Assyrian palace. In this part of the palace a lift still functions, installed in the

King's old age to help him to the upper floor when an old war wound made walking painful.

The palace is destined for a new life as a national museum, for which its towers, balconies and courtyards make it especially well suited. One day the visitor will walk through rooms steeped with the recent history of the kingdom as he looks back into the region's distant past.

Another historic area due to be incorporated into the modern life of the city is that surrounding the Masmak fort; here a civic centre is to be developed, with the old fort at its core. Masmak fort, in the heart of the busy shopping streets of the town centre, is dwarfed today by multi-storey concrete buildings, and given a somewhat incongruous air by the rows of large cars parked before its main gate. It is hard now to imagine that the fort once dominated its surroundings, that its towers could be seen by travellers coming into the city across the desert. It was built a century and a quarter ago and for over fifty years was a key stronghold in the city; today it is the oldest surviving building of importance in Riyadh.

In the early years of this century Masmak was the scene of dramatic and decisive events. To the right of the small door set in the main gate a spear head is buried in the wood; in the room to the left inside the gate there are bullet holes in the wall; brown stains on a wall in the front passageway are said to be from the blood of fallen defenders.

When the present century opened, Riyadh was governed from Hail and the Al Saud family were living in exile in Kuwait. In January 1902 a 22-year-old prince of the Al Saud, Abdul Aziz ibn Abd al Rahman, rode across the desert with a small group of followers, in the hope of regaining his family's usurped land. They slipped into the city of Riyadh one evening and made their way to a house opposite the fort. From its roof they climbed into the house of the governor Ajlan, only to find that he was spending the night in the Masmak fort. They spent a somewhat tense night, drinking coffee and eating dates, and as Abd al Aziz himself described it: 'We slept a little while . . . prayed the morning prayer, and sat thinking what we should do.'

At dawn when Ajlan and his retinue came out of the fort, Abd al Aziz and his companions attacked across the open square. Abdullah ibn Jiluwi, a cousin of Abd al Aziz, threw his spear at Ajlan but it missed and became embedded in the door. The defenders retreated back into the fort. Ajlan slipped through the door, but was closely pursued by Ibn Jiluwi who shot him dead in the room to the left of the doorway. The battle for the fort was

A STREET IN THE OLD PARTS OF RIYADH

soon over; no one at the time could have foreseen that the fruit of this hour's work was to be the Kingdom of Saudi Arabia.

Although the young prince Abd al Aziz was soon able to control the city of Riyadh, and to capture from the Turks the rich Hasa oasis over which he appointed his cousin Ibn Jiluwi as governor, he was still far from having recovered his family's ancient land. Arabia was divided into three separate states; that of the Sherif of Mecca in the west; of the Ibn Rashid with their capital at Hail in the north; and now that of Ibn Saud in the east. As the First World War dawned, the great powers wondered which of the three states to back. The Turks supported the Ibn Rashid and tried to dominate the Sherif of Mecca; the British negotiated with Ibn Saud but gave their main support to the Sherif. The three states seemed fairly evenly matched.

Abd al Aziz, however, was dreaming of a greater past. A century and a half earlier his family had been masters of all Arabia and of lands beyond as well. From their capital in Diriyah in the Wadi Hanifa, some 16 kilometres north of Riyadh, his ancestors had extended their sway and challenged the Turkish Empire. Their success was due to the alliance of two men, Muhammad ibn Saud and the religious leader, Muhammad ibn Abd al Wahhab, who had taken refuge in Diriyah. Sheikh Abd al Wahhab preached a return to the pure ways of the early days of Islam and condemned ostentation and un-Islamic rituals. The stringent demands of Abd al Wahhab's preaching were too much for certain people of his home town and they planned to kill him.

In Diriyah his alliance with Muhammad ibn Saud was sealed by the marriage of his daughter to Muhammad's son, and the forces of Diriyah set out to spread the teaching of Islam enunciated by Abd al Wahhab, with the active assistance of the Al Saud. It was the same invincible combination which had carried the tribes of Islam so far in the early days of the Arab conquests, and by the beginning of the nineteenth century it brought the Saudis to Mecca and Medina. This was more than the Sublime Porte could accept quietly and they requested their viceroy of Egypt, Muhammad Ali, to deal with the threat from Diriyah. Muhammad Ali was delighted, for this seemed to offer scope to expand his own domains, but warfare in Arabia proved tough and his troops were involved in years of fighting before eventually reaching Diriyah.

In 1818 however, after a five months' siege, the Al Saud were forced to surrender Diriyah and the Egyptian forces laid it waste. Buildings were mined, towers razed and palm trees chopped down. Today the old town of Diriyah stands as the invaders left it, silent on the banks of Wadi Hanifa. Its sandy streets and buildings and great city walls are there still, but derelict – here a gash torn by a mine, there a building totally collapsed. It is a romantic, evocative place to visit from Riyadh, peaceful in its desolation. The contrast between the jagged and broken mud buildings and the luscious green cultivation in the wadi below, the gentle thud-thud of pumps in the wadi gardens, an occasional small child whose family has made their home near the ruins, these are old Diriyah.

At its feet a new village has grown, guided by a modern Community Development Centre. The Centre provides agricultural advice and assistance, health care, literacy classes, cooking and

RUINS AT DIRIYAH

sewing classes, and a craft centre. The women weave bags and carpets, and make straw hats, baskets and mats; their products are sold through a permanent exhibition of handcrafts and agricultural exhibits. In a hut on the edge of the village I watched a woman weaving with the help of her two small daughters. In a corner of the hut her black tent was folded ready to leave at any time. Yes, she said the Centre was a great help to her but every now and then the desert called.

The desert called, too, to the descendants of the Al Saud who had re-established themselves in Riyadh nearby and who continued from there to control the districts around them. However, by the end of the nineteenth century their fortunes had ebbed: they had lost everything including Riyadh until the bold return of Abd al Aziz who, moving in the steps of his ancestors, set out once more to extend his domains. In 1921 he took Hail and in 1924 he took Mecca from the Sherif; the Asir was conquered in 1926, and possession of Najran in the extreme south-west confirmed in 1934. In 1932 the whole country of over 2 million square kilometres

ONE OF THE SMALLER CASTLES IN HAIL

became known as the Kingdom of Saudi Arabia.

The province of Nejd, in which Riyadh, Diriyah and Hail all lie, is the core of Saudi Arabia and the cradle of its ruling family. Control of Nejd was the main bone of contention between the Al Saud and the Ibn Rashid throughout the last century.

The rival city of Hail in the Jebel Shammar was visited by several foreigners in the past century, who all came away with strange tales to tell. Several of them were drawn to the region to buy horses, for central Arabia was the home of the pure Arabian from which the thoroughbreds of the West were reared. The Blunts, who visited Hail just a century ago, found the horses disappointing but were much impressed by the palace telephone, the first they had ever seen! Lady Anne Blunt told the terrible story of how the current Emir, Muhammad ibn Rashid, had killed his nephew, the ruling prince, then invited all his cousins to a meal and had them killed too. Charles Doughty, who also visited Hail about that time, wrote:

'And Mohammed fears! – the sword which has entered this princely house shall never depart from them.'

Hail today shows no sign of its disturbed past. It is a flourishing modern town with dual carriageways, new white buildings, and a modern airport. A sign in English at the entrance to the town, 'Welcome to Hail', would have surprised the Blunts or Charles Doughty. Another, in Korean, indicating I suppose some construction site, would have surprised them even more. A new sports centre and hotel have brought a further taste of the twentieth century.

The setting of Hail is as beautiful as it must always have been – against the jagged backdrop of the Jebel Shammar to the north, and with olive groves and palm gardens extending on either side. Steep, fertile valleys cut into the mountain range, within a few kilometres of the town, and offer a welcome green haven for Friday outings.

In the town itself a few mud-built castles are the only reminders of the past; the largest of the old castles have already been demolished to make way for development. Most impressive of those remaining are a square fort (once a barracks), known as the Kishla, and the beautiful castle of Ibn Jiluwi. The latter is strengthened by a number of round and square towers with crenellations and machicoulis, disposed it seems at random among the buildings. The Kishla on the other hand is constructed to a highly regular plan, with square towers at each corner and in the centre of each wall. Inside, its large courtyards are surrounded by colonnaded balconies at ground and first-floor level.

East of the Ibn Jiluwi castle is a district of old mud houses set among palm gardens. A feature of these houses was their brightly painted doors which can still be seen in some homes cut through for road development, and are on sale from time to time in the souq. The houses also had bands of sculpted patterns cut into the plaster and running round the walls or decorating storage niches. The people of the district found us as interesting as we found the buildings in the area; two little girls tugged shyly at our fair hair to 'see if it was real'. Where did we come from and how did we make it that colour? their mother asked.

Between Hail and Riyadh lies the rich agricultural district of Qasim, completely belying one's preconceptions of the desert of Nejd. True, great tongues of rolling red sand dunes extend way south from the Nafud desert, forming barriers to easy transport until asphalt roads were cut across them. At one such point where the road was incomplete for 10 kilometres, we were towed by a family of young men each driving a large Mercedes truck. They made the journey to Kuwait once or twice each week, taking farm produce from Qasim. Although only aged between eighteen and twenty-two years, they already owned two of the trucks and were hoping soon to buy more. They drove at night to avoid the heat and traffic, and handled their vehicles expertly in the deep sand.

Buraydah, whence they came, is the larger of Qasim's two towns and some 25 kilometres away from its twin, Unayzah. Both towns have been considerably modernized in recent years, now having many districts of new houses and wide modern roads. They show signs of traditional prosperity, however, in their extensive and attractive older districts, where streets of well-built and well-maintained mud houses show the plan of comfortable towns of the past century.

Delighted by these picturesque streets, we hurried in among the old houses of Buraydah, camera in hand, forgetting that western women friends who had visited the town some five years previously had thought it prudent to go veiled. We soon found that attitudes in Qasim have changed in recent years. A group of boys who watched us photographing begged us to stay till the evening in order to take pictures of their sister's wedding. This was typical of the friendliness which we met in the town and we were sad not to have time to accept their invitation.

The traditional houses in these towns are reminiscent of those of Riyadh, yet each place has a slightly different style overall. In Buraydah the houses have crowstep crenellations along the roof line and many have colonnaded balconies. Below the crenellations runs a line of inverted triangles which is also used to decorate the tapering round mud minarets of the town's old mosques. Unayzah's mud houses in general lack the crowstep crenellation, but are decorated instead with single pinnacles at the corners of the roofs. Many of their walls are pierced by triangular openings to admit the breeze, similar to those in the ruins of Diriyah.

In Unayzah palm gardens and buildings are closely intermingled and a large animal market is held in a shady palm grove just off the main square. On the other side of the square is one of the most charming little markets, in a narrow covered alley between two rows of colonnades. Here the women vendors sit cross legged on the ground to sell their wares, each one surrounded by piles of pots and pans and household goods, large boxes of biscuits, plastic sandals, or spices with their delicious heavy scent. Blind alleys run from the souq between smooth mud walls, culminating in carved but only slightly painted doorways.

The modern development of Unayzah and Buraydah has made

A STREET IN BURAYDAH

the towns comfortable to live in today, with electricity, schools, an agricultural institute, wide roads and so on. Many of the inhabitants are moving into new apartments in the towns or brightly painted villas in the suburbs. But it is the old districts which give the towns their charm, individual character and style. The memory which one carries away of these towns of the Qasim is of warm coloured mud buildings, each one different from its neighbours, of narrow shady lanes and of palm trees waving their fronds between the buildings.

2
The Heartland of Islam

Mecca and Medina are no ordinary cities. For a Muslim they are the goal of his aspirations, the places which he dreams of visiting as the culmination of his life's religious experience. It is, indeed, his religious duty to make a pilgrimage to Mecca once in his lifetime if he has the means to do so. Rich and poor alike, throughout the Muslim world, make every effort to complete at least one pilgrimage.

Mecca and Medina today are both by-passed by modern ring roads along which all non-Muslims must travel. The road which runs around the northern side of Medina passes close enough for travellers to be able to look across the buildings of the city and see the minarets of the Great Mosque. The Mecca by-pass, by contrast, makes a wide detour through the desert to the south.

I have not visited either Medina or Mecca, so any account of the towns which I might give would have to be by 'hear-say'. I shall leave descriptions of the cities themselves, therefore, to the increasingly numerous pilgrims of all races and tongues who have recently been within their precincts.

The cities lie a little inland from the Red Sea and about 450 kilometres apart. Mecca, which is some seventy kilometres inland from the large sea port of Jeddah, is cradled in the foothills of the Hejaz escarpment, among barren rocky hills and sandy valleys. Medina, further to the north, is about twice as far from the sea and among considerably higher mountains. In summer the heat is great in both towns for the sun reverberates off the barren rocks which remain hot even at night. In both places, however, ample water supplies have encouraged flourishing communities since early times. Mecca had become not only an important post on the incense caravan route but also a religious centre by the sixth century of our era.

The Prophet Muhammad was born in Mecca in 570 AD and started to preach there, but most of his fellow citizens would not heed him. In 622 he was obliged to flee from his home town and was invited to settle in the then Yathrib, which from that time became known as Al Medina al Munawwara ('The City of Light'); the dates of the Muslim lunar calendar are also counted from that year. The Prophet's move to Medina marks the true beginning of the spread of Islam and although his home town of Mecca also accepted the new faith during his life-time, he continued to live and finally died and was buried in Medina. Most pilgrims therefore include a visit to Medina within their pilgrimage to Mecca. Today, this is only a five- or six-hour car or coach journey; in the past it involved a week of hardship and privation by camel or on foot, travelling through the hot and humid coastal plain.

Mecca, as an ancient religious site, was already a centre of pilgrimage at the time of the Prophet. After the city accepted Islam its traditional pilgrimage was incorporated into the new faith and its importance greatly enhanced. The Ka'ba, an almost cubic structure, located at the centre of the Great Mosque, is the focal point to which Muslims in every corner of the world must face at prayer. In a corner of the Ka'ba is the Black Stone which marks the point of starting the circumambulation of the Ka'ba which forms an essential part of the pilgrimage ceremonies.

The pilgrimage ceremonies are closely related to the story of the Patriarch Abraham. Muslims believe that it was in Mecca that God ordered him to sacrifice his son and here that Satan tried to persuade him to disobey the orders of the Lord. They also believe that it was here that his second wife, Hagar, and her young son Ishmael, were cast out into the desert and were finally saved when the angel Gabriel showed them water at the well of Zamzam.

Today's pilgrims find the holy sites of Mecca and Medina much as they have been over the ages. They enter the sacred cities dressed in *ihram,* the special garment consisting of two unsewn strips of white material which gives all pilgrims, rich and poor alike, the same appearance as they come before their Lord. The impression made by so great a multitude gathered together to praise God is inspiring: 'Standing among that huge crowd at the pilgrimage, our thoughts and looks in unison, was the most wonderful experience of my life,' said one young, western-educated girl from Jeddah. When the throng of pilgrims move outside the town of Mecca, into the valley of Muna and on the plain of Arafat, they live in the same white pilgrim tents as their forebears.

The approaches to the pilgrimage, however, and the pilgrims' lodgings in Mecca, Medina and Jeddah, have seen vast changes in the past few years. Multi-lane highways with flyover bridges speed up the heavy traffic to the holy sites outside Mecca; in the city

PILGRIMS IN MECCA

itself a new Intercontinental Hotel offers luxurious accommodation to the well-to-do, while modern pilgrim hotels in Jeddah and Mecca provide clean, comfortable housing for the masses.

The Saudi Government goes to great trouble and expense to ensure a comfortable and epidemic-free pilgrimage. There has been a veritable explosion in the numbers of people making the journey each year, thanks largely to the fast, easy journeys offered by air travel. Today over a million pilgrims converge on Mecca, of which more than three-quarters of a million have come from outside Saudi Arabia. Strict health and visa controls, smooth traffic arrangements which have been greatly improved by the introduction of a fleet of large blue and white pilgrim buses, and the use of such modern methods of crowd control as helicopters, radio and television networks, all make for a safer, healthier pilgrimage.

In the past twenty years the numbers converging on Saudi Arabia for the *hajj* (pilgrimage) have increased from 200,000 to 800,000 or 900,000 in a peak year. The numbers arriving by sea, around 100,000, have remained constant. The new modern asphalt roads which now criss-cross the kingdom from all the major frontier posts have attracted far more overland travellers – an increase from 50,000 to nearly 300,000. For a month before the pilgrimage they can be seen arriving along all the main roads. The majority probably come by bus, their bundles of belongings piled up along the roof. Many more come in well-filled family cars, again often with their cases and bags on the roof. Cars and buses pull up by the roadside at prayer times, and the pilgrims alight to pray in the sand. From the distance they look like flocks of white birds as they kneel and rise again, their white garments flapping in the breeze. As they leave with elation after the pilgrimage, their cars and buses proudly fly the green pilgrims' flags from the wings and roof racks.

By far the most startling change, however, has been in the numbers arriving by air, which have leapt from around 40,000 to nearly 500,000. Jeddah's airport has been practically overwhelmed every year at pilgrimage time by the seemingly endless arrival of families from distant lands, the old grandparents nursing fretful babies while the younger men of the family try to locate their baggage, work out the formalities, and find their way to the hotel accommodation beside the airport.

A miracle of organization, it seems, has enabled this small airport to handle a flight every three minutes during *hajj* time with a clear accident record. The large new Jeddah airport, nearing completion at the time of writing, lies to the north of Jeddah and has direct road access to both Mecca and Medina without the need for pilgrims to

A WOMAN SITTING IN THE SHADE

drive first through the busy streets. Its fine *hajj* terminal, for the exclusive use of pilgrims, offers a luxurious introduction to Saudi Arabia.

In previous centuries the pilgrimage to Mecca was a very different experience and infinitely more taxing. While some pilgrims must always have arrived at Jeddah, the seaport to Mecca, after a more or less comfortable journey by sea, the majority travelled overland. They gathered in the capitals of neighbouring Muslim countries, in Cairo, Damascus and Baghdad, waiting until the great caravan with its armed guards was ready to move off.

The wealthy rode on camels, donkeys or in litters swaying on camel back; the poor walked. The immense columns moved ahead at a rate of some 20–30 kilometres a day, stopping at night under the protection of a fort or guard house, beside a well. At these stopping places they could buy provisions from the local bedouin, and above all they could obtain water.

In the early centuries of Islam a great pilgrim route was organized across the central deserts of Arabia, from Kufa near Baghdad to Mecca and Medina. This was already in use in the first century of Islam and some of its major stations, such as Fayd near Hail, were fortified and equipped with facilities. During the following two centuries, however, in the golden age of the Abbasid caliphate in

Baghdad, extensive works were undertaken whose remains can still be traced along the whole length of the route. Many of the Abbasid caliphs made the pilgrimage in person, and each added his share of improvements: a stretch of the route would be cleared of boulders, a cutting made through the hills, and milestones set up. Most important was the provision of way stations where pilgrims could pass the night in security and, vital to their survival, could rely on obtaining water.

The greatest benefactors to the pilgrims from Baghdad were the Caliph Harun al Rashid, of *Arabian Nights* fame, and his cousin wife, Queen Zubaydah. Both made numerous pilgrimages to Mecca, sometimes even travelling on foot with their poorest subjects. Queen Zubaydah devoted the later years of her life to improving the route, particularly by the provision of water sources between the major stations, where they would be of most help to the poor who must travel slowly, and at Mecca itself.

Today most of the stations along this route are simply mounds of sand and ruins, the great cisterns are silted and the tracks are trodden only by an occasional bedouin and his herd. Many of the wells, however, have continued to provide water over the centuries and are still used by the bedouin. Two of the cisterns were cleared out and renovated in 1973, and can be easily visited for they are only a few hours' drive across the desert north of Taif.

One of these way stations is in the Wadi al Aqiq, its ruins lying in the shade of great trees and showing the outlines of extensive buildings, caravanserais, houses and a small dam across the wadi. On one bank of the wadi is a large square cistern surrounded by a modern wall, some 50 metres along each side. A flight of steep steps descends into the water all round the pool and the area is always thronged with bedouin who come with their pickup trucks, tankers and lorries to collect their water supplies from this ample source. Swallows skim across the surface of the cistern; trees in the wadi alongside it are covered in spring with pink flowers. It must have offered a welcome resting place to pilgrims crossing the blazing desert in the past, just as it does to the modern traveller today.

Some 18 kilometres east of this cistern is the even more interesting watering station of Birkat al Khuraba. Here a very large circular cistern has been cleaned and repaired, and alongside it are a large oblong settling tank and a small domed guard house straddling the bank between the two pools. Two arched tunnels run under the guard house and link the pools, each of which is surrounded by the same kind of steep steps as at Wadi al Aqiq. During a severe drought in 1977 the pools were emptied and it was possible to descend to the

READING ON THE STAIRS

bottom. They are about 8 metres deep and the diameter of the circular pool at its base is 44 metres, its circumference at ground level is almost 200 metres and it is one of the largest pools on the Darb Zubaydah. Even the oblong pool. which is fed by a canal at ground level, is some 27 by 40 metres. These cisterns normally provide the major water source for the bedouin of the region.

The other famous ancient pilgrim route ran through slightly less arid terrain, and waterworks on the scale of those of the Darb Zubaydah were generally not necessary. This is a route whose antiquity goes back into the mists of time. It passes through the beautiful mountainous country of the northern Hejaz, and was the way taken by the huge pilgrim caravans which started out each year from Damascus and Cairo. Unlike the Darb Zubaydah, which was largely abandoned in medieval times, this route was used until the present century and there are many travellers' accounts of the experiences of the pilgrim caravans.

Here again a safe night's lodging was a first essential. Large stone forts were constructed at numerous points along the route in the sixteenth and seventeenth centuries, around which the pilgrims set up their tents; the forts also guarded wells and small cisterns for the pilgrims' use. A hundred years ago an Englishman, Charles Doughty, travelled with the pilgrim caravan from Damascus as far as Al Ula. He rode alongside 6,000 pilgrims in a column with 10,000 camels. At Medain Salih, site of the famous Nabataean ruins, he left the caravan in order to stay at the fort which he describes thus: 'We came marching over the loamy plain to Medain Salih . . . where the caravan arriving was saluted with many rounds from the field pieces and we alighted at our encampment of white tents, pitched a little before the kella (fort) . . . a tower seventy feet upon a side, square built.'

The fort still stands today, much as Doughty knew it, but empty – its cistern dry, its well used only by a few local cultivators. One wall has partly collapsed and it is possible to step into the central courtyard, look up to the gallery above and the rooms where the garrison slept, and see the smoke-blackened arches under which they built their fires.

Near the fort are the ruins of more recent structures, the buildings of a large railway station which seem oddly out of place in this remote and ancient spot. An oval water tower also stands close by. A few yards away a 1908 railway engine sits intact in a crumbling engine shed; beyond are the sidings with the skeletons of coaches, and the numerous red-roofed buildings of a substantial station on the Hejaz railway.

The railway was proposed by the Sultan Abdul Hamid in 1900 and a subscription was raised from Muslim countries whose pilgrims it was to carry. The rails, rolling stock and equipment were of cosmopolitan manufacture and brought from many countries: red curved tiles from Marseilles, rails from Turkey and Maryland, a carriage from Belgium and an engine from Scotland which still stand along the track. The charming little pink stone stations were designed by German engineers; they served a double purpose as miniature forts, protecting the line and the Turkish troop trains which found it increasingly useful as the First World War engulfed the Middle East.

With the Arab revolt against the Turks the Hejaz railway became an obvious target. It was constantly attacked in the later years of

TURKISH STATION ALONG THE HEJAZ RAILWAY

the war by the local tribes aided by Lawrence of Arabia. Their handiwork is still plainly seen in the grotesquely twisted rails which arch in the air a little to the south of Al Ula, and the tender lying on its side near the track, its wheels some yards away. In *Seven Pillars of Wisdom,* T. E. Lawrence describes mining the track between Al Ula and Medina: 'At random I pitched on kilometre 1121 from Damascus . . . it was a complicated mine, with a central trigger to fire simultaneous charges thirty yards apart; we hoped in this way to get the locomotive whether it was going north or south.'

Some patching-up was done, and an occasional train made the trip to Amman in the early 1920s, but effectively this beautifully built railway, with its steel sleepers and well-laid embankment, died only a decade after it was completed. Since then its resurrection has often been contemplated, and a considerable amount of preparatory work was done in the 1960s, when sleepers and tracks were raised and stacked for relaying, and culverts were repaired or reconstructed. Then the work was abandoned. Today the reopening of the Hejaz railway is again under consideration, as part of a scheme to create a national railway network. Meanwhile new asphalt roads are being laid parallel to the old railway tracks and sections of the old pilgrim way can already be covered comfortably by car.

3
Jeddah
the Commercial Capital

'I found more than twenty sacks full of these old business letters in my grandfather's great house,' commented a young man from one of Jeddah's long-established business families. The big house was abandoned now, let off in tenements and with some of its main reception rooms already in ruins. Abd al Rahman had preserved some of the letters but in his small modern apartment he sadly could not keep them all.

The letters and bills were in many languages: they referred to goods shipped from Scotland, from India, from Turkey or France. 'From Greenwell Bros., Butchers, Sunderland, 1874. Account for supplying SS *Anglesey* with meat: £21.9.10.' There were bills for spice, being the balance of goods from the SS *Ulysses*, stranded in Jeddah in 1875; for hardwood shipped from East Africa; for porcelain brought from China; compensation for a damaged cargo here, proceeds from the sale of goods there. This was the stuff of the trade directed from the office in the rambling old house in the heart of the souq.

Today the goods arriving hourly at Jeddah port and airport have changed: cars, heavy equipment, machinery, frozen foods, or building materials form the basis of twentieth-century trade. The patriarch of the family no longer sits in his office by the huge entrance gate of the extended family home, his money and papers in the great iron safe by his side. Today his grandsons enjoy modern offices, the desks equipped with a battery of telephones; telex messages are brought in throughout the day, bills paid by cheque, and the millions arising from the trading boom which started in the 1970s are stowed safely in one of the city's many banks.

Despite these changes in style and emphasis, and despite the amazing building boom of the past decade, the spirit of Jeddah has not changed. Its *raison d'être* as the kingdom's main port and trading city, and as the gateway to Mecca and starting point of the pilgrimage, remain as they always were. The scale, though, has altered beyond belief and the means of dealing with it are being rapidly transformed to keep pace.

Jeddah had grown to a city of three-quarters of a million people by the late 1970s, from a town of 200,000 ten years previously. Her primary gateway to the world remains her seaport, now a major harbour handling thousands of tons of cargo each day. In centuries past, shallow-draught wooden sailing ships tied up in the sheltered lagoon on the northern side of the old town, in front of the site where the attractive modern building of the Ministry of Foreign Affairs now stands. Gradually a harbour was developed due west of the town and in 1948 the old city walls were pulled down to provide fill for the construction of the causeway leading to the modern deep-water quays.

The port was continuously enlarged and kept pace with the country's needs until 1974 when imports suddenly escalated and queues of ships waiting to discharge their cargoes began to form in the roadsteads. For a year or so their lights out to sea at night began to rival those of the city on land. However, the goods were urgently needed for the kingdom's development programme; radical solutions were needed and found. For a time the sight of a fleet of helicopters, hovering over the port like giant dragonflies then suddenly flying off with a load of cement dangling from the ends of their long cables, was commonplace in Jeddah's seascape. These and other administrative and development efforts brought the port's activities into top gear; the backlog of shipping was cleared and has not reappeared.

During the port's years of crisis on the mercantile side, it could never close its doors to the thousands of pilgrims who arrive each year to make the pilgrimage to Mecca. While cargo ships had to wait their turn in the hot and sultry roadsteads, the pilgrim ships were brought straight in to the special pilgrim terminal, most elegant of the port's numerous buildings, and – their formalities completed – transported from there to the pilgrim hotel just outside the harbour gates.

Handling the pilgrim traffic is no longer the major problem for the Jeddah port that it is for the airport, since the numbers arriving by sea are now fairly static. The airport, on the contrary, has had to cope with the expansion of pilgrim traffic previously described. Moreover, pilgrims are not the only air travellers whose numbers have increased. Thirty years ago the airport in the Kandara district was a quiet little runway outside the town. Today the city has expanded around three sides of the airport and with the provision of new asphalt roads to the east, is rapidly extending around that side also. Planes arrive and take off continually throughout the day

A STREET CORNER IN JEDDAH

and new lounges became essential in the mid-1970s despite the imminent opening of the major new airport to the north.

When I first drove into Jeddah in 1974 this new airport seemed very remote from the town, about 20 kilometres out in the desert to the north. A herd of camels grazed just outside its perimeter fence, and the only buildings in sight were those of the cement factory. Three years later the new airport was linked to Jeddah by an almost uninterrupted line of buildings which were beginning to extend westward to the sea and eastward to the foothills. Even before its runways opened to planes the airport was virtually a part of the town.

The town is destined to extend further north still, beyond the airport and as far as the Creek, Sharm Obhur, the city's favourite seaside resort. The drawings of the town plan show a network of roads, ruled in parallel lines across the desert, and blocked in with patches of different colours to denote high- or low-density housing, industrial areas, or regions for recreation and open space. On the plan it all seems very logical and normal, but in reality the effect of such rapid development is almost surrealistic: three months after driving along a familiar desert track through an empty landscape we follow the same route and can scarcely believe that the track is a dual-carriageway asphalt road, estates of pre-fabricated houses are nearing completion on either side, a batching plant is in full swing, huge sewerage pipes are already disappearing underground and conventional houses are rising rapidly out of the ground. Have we taken the wrong route? we ask bemused – such transformation cannot be real. But it is, and this is the essence of Jeddah in the second half of the twentieth century.

The change has been most marked in the past few years but does not surprise the city's permanent residents who have lived with change all their lives. In the well-developed, almost central district of Sharafiya, one householder looks round at the lofty shady trees and well-established gardens and houses of this 'older' area. 'When we first built here twenty years ago the desert was at our gate and we used to watch the gazelles outside our garden walls,' she says. Today the desert is 12 kilometres away and the only gazelles are those kept as pets in her neighbours' gardens. On the Mecca road a young woman looks out across the miles of buildings from the balcony of the large house where she was brought up. Cars thunder past non-stop on the six-lane highway outside. 'As children we used to stand on this balcony and watch the pilgrims riding past on camels to Mecca. Sometimes the bedouin galloped by and we tried to guess which camel would win.'

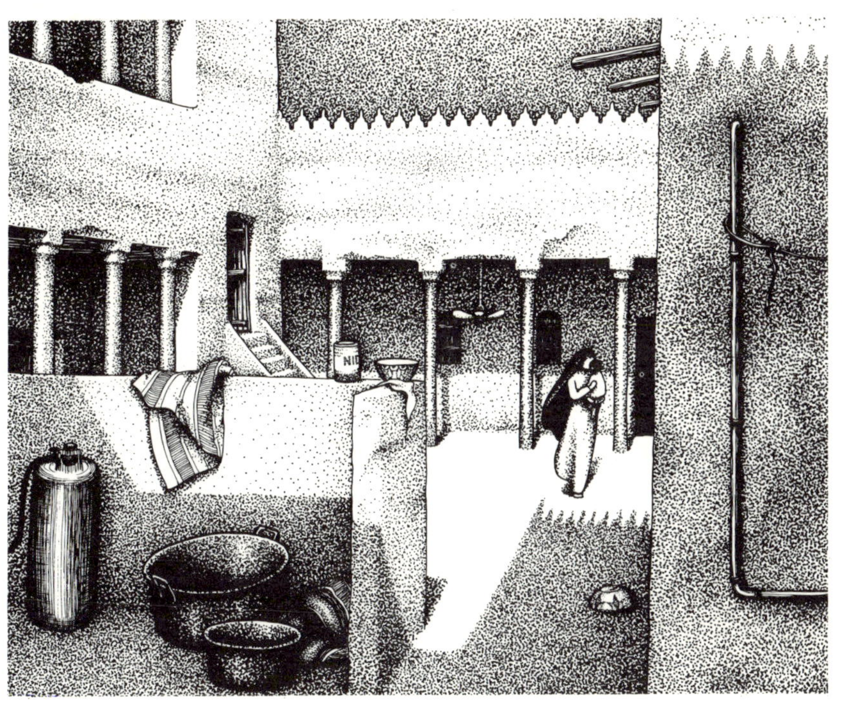

COURTYARD OF A NEJDI HOUSE

The inhabitants have lost the fresh air and open spaces of a small town and as their city grows it becomes more and more important to plan for recreation. The town's major asset is the Red Sea which glows in the evening under the bright red sunsets that seem to justify its name. The heat of the town lessens slightly on the shore, where a cooling breeze frequently blows off the water. In the past the houses were built to the water's edge, but today the shore line recedes each year as more land is reclaimed for development. Tomorrow the new coast line will be available to all as a Corniche road is built all along the shore from the town centre to north of the Creek. An almost continuous line of gardens, small parks and water resorts will be developed between the road and the sea, offering scope for those family picnics by the water, so much beloved of Jeddawis.

The sea shore beyond the building sites is delightful. A short stretch of soft sand leads across a line of stranded sea shells (some of which get up and scurry away – the homes of hermit crabs), along the high-water mark to warm shallow waters. This shallow stretch extends for 100 metres or more out to sea, to a line of breakers roaring white-crested surf on windy days, or a gentle ripple when the water is calm. This line marks the coral reef, imperceptible on the surface, an enchanted world of brilliant colour below the water.

The Red Sea coral reef, running all along the west coast of Saudi Arabia, is one of the richest reefs in the world, comparable to the Great Barrier Reef off Australia. The abrupt rocky cliff, which descends hundreds of metres into the murky depths, is clad with many forms of coral, some in beautiful shades of pink or mauve. All along the cliff face swarms of fish of all sizes, shapes and colours, swirl and turn. The smaller golden, red or orange varieties sparkle in the rays of sunlight which penetrate some way below the surface. Further down a huge dark shape may betray a shark or barracuda. On windy days the upper levels of the sea move with the motion of the waves and the fish swing uncomfortably from side to side.

It is a diver's paradise, for the varieties of fish run into hundreds and the types change as the diver swims deeper down the cliff. The wide range of Red Sea shells is another attraction, and includes many forms of cowrie. Indiscriminate collecting of shells and coral is sadly depleting the reef near the city, and spear guns could endanger some species of fish. But so far the Red Sea has proved a haven for species threatened with extinction elsewhere. Several types of turtle still breed on sandy islets here; the huge dugong, origin of the ancient mermaid legend, still comes in to browse on sea grasses in the quiet creeks further along the shore. Studies have been made with a view to conserving this rich marine life.

The surface of the sea provides just as much scope for recreation as do its depths. With water that is always warm, and in summer approaches the temperature of a bath, sports which elsewhere can only be regarded as spartan become a real pleasure. The Creek has been developed over the years as the main water-sports resort since its sheltered waters, protected by the reef, are safe from all but stone fish. Here waterskiers flash to and fro, sailing boats scud across the surface in the strong winds at midday, motor boats roar past with their strong bow wave, and occasionally one of the coastguards' hovercraft makes a stately progress between the shores.

Larger pleasure boats set out from here on fishing trips into the deep sea or along the coast to islands further north. Fishing with

DHOWS AGAINST THE SUNSET

rod and line is a popular sport as well as a means of livelihood in the Red Sea. On Jeddah's sea front one still sees some of the old wooden dhows of the fishermen and, in the evening, men wading out in the shallows to fish with cast nets. The dhows, however, already look like relics from the past, dwarfed by the huge ships and cranes of the modern harbour behind them, just as the houses of old Jeddah on their other side are dwarfed by the new high-rise buildings with their soaring cranes along the sea front.

The heart of the city is here at the centre, on the sea shore, in the district which was once enclosed by the old walls. This is the historic site of the port which has stood here for some two thousand years. The small, densely built area encloses the traditional alleys and houses of the old town, the crowded, covered lanes of the souq, and the intense activity of the business centre. Thirty years ago the old houses lined the sea front and were closely packed inland from there, but the sea-front area has long been cleared of old buildings

THE OLD SOUQ IN JEDDAH

and King Abdul Aziz Street, near the shore, is lined with modern constructions. Most impressive of these is the multi-storey apartment and office block of the Queen's Building. The high apartment tower and the curving glass façade of the lower office section are landmarks of the city, seen both from the sea and from inland.

Below them are the sandy lanes lit at night by gas lamps hung from wooden gibbets, with traditional coral houses of old Jeddah. In their day these old houses seemed very tall too, rising four or five storeys and shading completely the narrow lanes between them. These coral buildings are special to the western province, to Jeddah, Mecca, Taif and Yanbu and, on the other side of the Red Sea, to the island of Suakin on which Hejazi merchants built themselves another town.

The main building material for the sea-shore houses was the dead coral rag which lines the shore. This porous building material was held by tie beams and the ceilings were supported on round beams. The roofs of the houses were always flat, surrounded by stone walls or wooden balustrades, and provided living accommodation which would catch the breezes from the sea. In summer the whole family slept on the open roof at night. 'We lay looking up at the stars and listening to stories told to all the children of the family by an old negro woman,' one merchant recounted. 'I feel my own children miss something, in our small air-conditioned villa.'

The interior of the houses was designed for coolness also, and thick walls and glassless windows kept the temperature down even in summer. The most characteristic feature is the treatment of the windows, many of which are enclosed in projecting wooden balconies. These balconies are made up of open trellis-work sections which allow the breeze to pass through and enable the inhabitants to look out without being seen themselves from the street. They are called *roshan* in the Hejaz and closely resemble the *mashrabiya* windows of old Cairo.

Inside the rooms a wide stone bench still runs along the walls. Rugs and cushions were laid along this bench to provide seating, or sleeping space in winter. Cushions were also placed in the projecting balconies, the coolest place of all to sit. The sun's rays slant through the balconies' screens, casting patterns of light and shade on the floors of the high-ceilinged rooms. In the slight breeze, specks of dust swirl in the sun's beams, producing a peaceful and sleepy atmosphere, very different from the hum of the modern air-conditioner and the blast of cold air blowing from it.

The houses, with their numerous storeys and steep, narrow staircases, were extended homes in which each branch of the family had its own apartments, while the whole family shared the main large reception rooms. Usually all the families ate together in the evening, the meal being prepared in a large central kitchen.

Best preserved of Jeddah's old houses today is the Nassif house in Shariya al Alawi, which is being restored by the government for use as a museum. In front of the house a large tree spreads its shade, today in no way exceptional but once the only tree in Jeddah. The story is told of a gentleman from India who was invited to stay in the great house by the hospitable Nassif family. On leaving he realized that he had forgotten his host's name and address, but his letter of thanks, addressed simply to 'The House by the Tree', arrived without delay.

The Nassif house is somewhat different from the usual design for it has two wide staircases sweeping up to each floor. The master of the home, in the past, was accustomed to ride straight up to his sitting room, handing his horse to a groom at the door. It is said that when King Abd al Aziz stayed in the house he favoured a belvedere room on the roof, at that time the highest point in Jeddah. Dispatch riders on racing camels would rush up the numerous flights of stairs and couch their mounts on the roof!

The great merchant families who lived in these old houses had come from many parts of the Arab world. Merchants from Syria, Egypt, the Hadramaut and Oman settled down side by side with others from Persia or India, and of course from the inland towns and deserts of Arabia itself. They gave the city a cosmopolitan air rather different from that of the rest of the country. Today, after several generations in Jeddah, the families have become completely Saudi but continue to work with their own relatives or with other families to whom they are related by marriage.

Most merchant families today run a major company involved in modern trade or development, or else a series of companies with related activities. Many of them have a branch in Riyadh or Dammam, to which they send a younger member of the family as manager, and most of them also provide the government service with one or two of their brighter young men. In a way this represents a financial sacrifice for the family, whose members could certainly earn more as businessmen than as government officials. But many families feel it is their duty. They like to be part of the modern state, not only as businessmen but at the heart of the government machine as well.

4
Life in the Cities

The quiet walled desert towns of thirty years ago have not grown into easygoing market towns, as for a while it seemed they might. Suddenly the pace of development has caught them in a whirlwind. They have become magnets for those leading the lonely life of the bedouin or the unchanging existence of the little oases, and their population has increased tenfold.

Over the past few decades a young man from a desert or village family might move into the city, staying with relatives and finding work alongside them. When he could afford a place of his own he would send for his wife and children to join him. An unmarried young man might ask his sisters to come and keep house for him, though the father would often require some persuading to agree to this. A sudden need for medical or dental treatment might often convince the old man that his son's offer was worth accepting, at least for the time being. Once departed, the young people rarely returned.

Many of these new city dwellers were ambitious. Some went to night school and thus were able to move on to office jobs. Many others, particularly those of bedouin origin, saw no attraction in being tied to a desk all day. Driving a vehicle had far more appeal; large numbers acquired their own car and became taxi drivers.

They reached the cities at the start of the great traffic boom and supplied a needed service. Streets and houses were spreading ever further from the town centre, and in the early 1970s only a relatively small percentage of the population owned their own cars; many city streets were still quiet sand tracks.

In the past few years the change in the city streets has been overwhelming. Cars and trucks vied with construction materials in the great import boom of 1975-76; soon it seemed that nearly every family owned one. While it is splendid to have a vehicle oneself, it is less agreeable to find all one's neighbours driving too. Sandy lanes became dust bowls, horns blared throughout the day and night, traffic snarl-ups proliferated and the ten-minute journey to work began to take half an hour or more.

Town planners had foreseen an increase in traffic though hardly to such an extent; work on the roads was already under way. The sandy lanes disappeared as even small side streets were asphalted; main roads became one-way thoroughfares, new dual carriageways were cut through populous districts. The wider roads led to faster driving and at crossroads still there were traffic pile-ups and collisions. The traffic problems could not easily be solved overnight. Numerous new flyovers and ring roads, however, opened in the late 1970s (especially in Riyadh), have helped to ease the situation.

While the city roads themselves are heavily used, the vehicles on them are also pressed into intensive service. Saudis really enjoy vehicles. They are always ready to dive under the bonnet and tinker with the engine when things go wrong; they manage to keep their vehicles going in the remote desert and to cross difficult sand tracks in pick-ups and even ordinary saloon cars. Whenever we have had a breakdown out in the country a group has always gathered, eager to help fix the trouble, push the vehicle out of the sand, or simply offer advice.

In the cities, the dense and hectic traffic accompanies a hectic pace of life. Change and development are all around. Every street in the 1970s had drains and cables laid, its surface asphalted, a pavement built, street lighting installed; empty plots became construction sites and any strip or corner of bare earth a garden, in the drive for 'beautification'. New suburbs and even whole new towns sprang up, if not overnight at least over the course of a year. For the residents life could be confusing: a friend's house could not be found because a whole series of new roads had been built around it; their telephone cable might be cut by road works and sometimes their electricity or water went the same way. But gradually the streets sorted themselves out: suddenly it was possible to drive straight through on a rapid highway instead of waiting, steaming, in a traffic jam; suddenly the messy building plot became an elegant villa; gradually, alongside the roads, the poor little plants, battered by the wind, sun and goats, flourished into brightly flowering shrubs. For a visitor returning after two or three years it was like coming to an unknown town.

The pressure of work has escalated with the rapid development. The vision of a gentle existence in Saudi cities has evaporated like a mirage and most people find themselves working harder than they ever have in Jeddah, Riyadh or Dammam. Offices open at 8 am and close at 2 pm; most businesses open again around 4.30 pm and keep working until late in the evening.

The pattern of work in Saudi offices is partly super-modern,

OLD MAN WALKING THROUGH A QUIET NEIGHBOURHOOD

partly traditional. Telexes hum, a battery of telephones on the desk keeps the official or businessman in contact not only with other Saudi cities but with New York, London, Tokyo, Zurich and Rome. Juggling telephones lodged between shoulder and ear has become a peculiarly Saudi art. Deals worth thousands, maybe millions of pounds are at stake.

Yet at the same time the old courtesies must be maintained. The office door is open to all comers and in many offices a nerveracking throng presses in, filling the seats around the wall. Each newcomer is greeted, offered tea or coffee, his petition heard, considered and dealt with, his file studied, his papers signed. And all the time the telephones ring and messengers come in and out with notes which must be read and answered.

A few very senior offices are now guarded by a secretary in an outer office who sifts through the crowd, and there the hubbub abates. Yet even so it is still surprisingly easy to see the busiest and most distinguished Saudis; they have not yet lost the common touch, but the cost in time and effort is heavy. As one official remarked, he worked an American-style day and a Saudi evening and he too now boasted an ulcer.

Relaxation at night is often in the form of dinner parties, either for men only or in a small mixed company of close friends or relatives. Such parties tend to start late and dinner is often served around midnight. 'Much better than it used to be, though, when we ate at 1 am or later,' a Saudi will tell you. From the official, who must be at his desk at 8 am, this comes with a sigh of relief. The businessman will usually allow himself an extra hour or two in bed in the morning on such occasions.

Both businessmen and officials, as well as their families, are saved by a siesta in the afternoon. Life comes to a halt in Saudi Arabia between 3 pm and 4.30 pm and one is definitely not popular if one chooses to telephone at such a time. When the sleepers wake the heat of the day is over; the men go back to work refreshed and the children sit down to their homework. The siesta brings a new lease of life, and is particularly cherished by shopkeepers and businessmen who may then work on until 9 or 10 pm. These evening hours are the pleasantest of the day: the shopping streets fill with people, men take their wives out to the souq, the crowds drift contentedly along enjoying the relative cool.

For a businessman this is often the time when he can best tackle his own work. Callers are fewer at night and at last he has his office to himself. He can be alone now with his relatives who are in business with him and with whom he will probably dine once the office doors are closed. Most businesses are family affairs and even an outlying branch in one of the other cities will probably be run by a brother or a cousin. They feel lonely at first but eventually establish their own branch of the family in their distant home.

Most of these families carefully raise their sons to come into the business when they are adult. In the shops young boys often help to serve; in the big businesses the sons may work in the various departments throughout their long summer holidays. As they grow older they are taught other useful skills; languages are the first of these, for Saudis trade with all parts of the world. The small children of wealthy families may have English nannies or go to Saudi nursery schools where English is taught. When they are ten or eleven many are sent to summer school in England, followed a year or so later by summers in Switzerland, France or Germany. Later they may take courses in economics or business studies at an American university, often staying to complete a PhD. Skills are distributed around the family to forge a powerful team.

Private life is equally family-centred in Saudi Arabia, In the past people lived almost exclusively within their own families, in extended-family houses in the towns and villages, or in family camping groups in the desert. Today this intense family closeness has been somewhat dispersed: the great houses in the towns have been abandoned for

A LITTLE GIRL DOING HER HOMEWORK

modern, single-family villas; many of the desert and village people have started a new life in the cities and have not always been able to bring all the family with them.

Despite all this, however, relatives still like to build their new homes close to each other, in the same district or even in the same walled compound. Thus they can enjoy the best of both worlds: the privacy to do as they like within the nuclear family, and the company and support of the extended family. 'A united family is a strong family,' remarked one Jeddah merchant who was building a family compound. In such a setting communal reception rooms are shared by all; often everyone gathers for evening and weekend meals.

A young foreign wife in a Saudi family finds it a good system: 'When I first arrived I wanted to build a little house for us away from the others. How lucky we did not have the money then. Two or three years later, when we could afford it, we built in the family compound. Now I have no baby sitting problems, I am never lonely yet I can be by myself when I want to.'

Children and old people have a particularly happy life in the extended family. The old have a position of considerable prestige: they remain very much at the head of the family, on whom the young make frequent calls ('Sorry I am late,' says a senior official. 'I had not seen my father for two days so I had to drop in on the way here.'). They are surrounded by several generations of young descendants, and when an old man or woman dies they are genuinely mourned; it is the loss of a corner stone of the clan.

The young children are spoilt by grandparents, aunts, uncles and cousins, who all carry the little ones around and make a great fuss of them. As they grow they enjoy continuous company from cousins among whom affections may develop which will lead to marriage in the future. The preferred match for a Saudi child is still with a cousin. This can often be happily arranged when families have lived together from childhood.

While an open-plan life within the extended family is popular, seclusion from the outside world is firmly sought. Most houses have high walls around their gardens; smaller homes may have virtually windowless walls onto the street and a sheltered courtyard in the middle. The family stay in their own garden or yard; the street is not a social centre as it is in some hot countries.

Entertainment for women and children must be mostly within their own homes. There are no public cinemas or theatres, no cafés where they might go with other women and children. With the spread of education, the lives of women have changed considerably over the past few decades, however. Air conditioning encourages greater activity in the house, and television has opened windows to the outside world – it is immensely popular with rich and poor alike, and in the humbler homes the television set is often placed in the yard at night where there is space for relatives in the cool evening.

Videotape libraries hire out colour films to the well-to-do. In the late afternoon many mothers and their children sit and watch a film with family friends, or they may enjoy one of the electronic games of football or tennis which are played onto the television set. In the

AN EVENING IN FRONT OF THE TV

evenings card games are popular with all the family.

The telephone has brought a welcome change to the lives of many city women. They can chat with their women friends all day (for local calls are free). Relatives in Riyadh, Jeddah or al Khobar can be called by direct dialling and many families now make regular weekly calls to student sons and daughters in the United States or Europe.

Study is an important part of life for most city children, girls as well as boys. School examinations must be passed each year if the child is to continue. Homework is taken seriously, especially by the girls who tend to outshine their brothers at exam time. Boys have attended school for many years and now over half a million boys are in school. Girls' schools were first opened in the early 1960s and in less than two decades have expanded to take more than a quarter of a million girls. Families are very eager to educate their daughters and the number of girls attending Saudi universities increased dramatically in the late 1970s.

Like the boys, many girls now also enjoy higher studies abroad, especially when they have a young student husband at university in the United States or Europe. People say that one of a young man's greatest assets in the search for a beautiful and intelligent wife is a place at a foreign university where she too may have a chance to study.

Girls are just beginning to play a role in the country's economy where their talents could be useful, for there is a great need for skilled Saudi labour. The government actively encourages them to take jobs as teachers in girls' schools and colleges, and as nurses and doctors in hospitals for women and children. A few are beginning to look further afield in their choice of work, but they are officially restricted to working in an all-female environment. Women's welfare associations in the cities offer an opportunity for charitable work with orphans and needy families, and give courses in such practical skills as sewing, typewriting and adult literacy.

Just as study and work outside the home are becoming increasingly widespread, so also are outside leisure pursuits. For men there have long been the traditional cafés with their high benches set outside on the pavement. Here the men gather, sitting cross-legged on the wide seats, to drink tea from little glass cups, smoke a hubble-bubble pipe (*nargileh*), and discuss the affairs of the day. Television now provides an added attraction in some cafés.

More popular nowadays is the ubiquitous sport of football which has captivated the young in city and countryside alike. Any spare plot of ground can be used as a pitch and as these are being swallowed up in housing developments, the government is providing football clubs and stadia to promote higher standards of play. The passion to excel in this sport exceeds all others and British trainers have been hired to bring up promising young players from the grass roots, and to forge a national team.

On a more light-hearted level, permanent fun fairs known as Luna Parks are a magnet to draw all the family. The Luna Parks reserve some evenings for men, some for women only, and some for families. Most popular are the family nights when excited children run about in their best clothes, the little girls in long glittery dresses and boys in smart white *thawbs;* on these nights an unaccompanied male is not admitted.

The pleasure of the children is matched by that of the teenagers, who eagerly make for the bumper cars which are always crowded. One can see black-veiled girls, eye slits decorated with gold sequins, driving with élan.

The rise in car ownership in the past few years has facilitated another kind of family outing, the evening picnic. Some families like to drive out of the city into the desert to spend their Fridays. By far the greater number, however, have no desire for such solitude. They simply like to drive to the suburbs (and in Jeddah this is always the new Corniche Road running along the seashore).

At weekends the place is packed with people, happy to have

A BAKERY

others close by. A Saudi friend once remarked that he could not see what we saw in the desert. 'Marvellous to get away from everyone,' we explained. 'But that is the last thing we want,' he said. 'We have spent centuries of loneliness in the desert; now we want to be where the people are, to be part of the crowd.'

5
Mountains of the South West

The mountains of the escarpment rise high above the steaming plain bordering the Red Sea along the south-west coast of Saudi Arabia. Due east of Mecca and some 140 kilometres inland from Jeddah, a wall of mountains rises abruptly; as one drives up and up the air becomes fresh, cool and dry. Suddenly it is a pleasure to breathe. A few kilometres east of the cliff top the road rises over a saddle in the hills and there below the town of Taif is spread among the rocky outcrops, beautiful in the clear atmosphere 1700 metres above sea level.

The approach to the town from the east, while less dramatic than that from the west, is almost equally welcoming. The main road from Riyadh runs across some 800 kilometres of monotonous, arid gravel plain, the least interesting of desert scenery. Finally, as it approaches Taif, the desert becomes greener, clad with scrubby little acacia bushes which are much relished, it seems, by the numerous herds of camels habitually grazing there. Then the road cuts through a rocky ridge, once guarded by forts long since in ruins, and the desolate wilderness is left behind. Here are real trees, some cultivation, soon the airport and the strip building which heralds the approach of a major town.

The countryside around Taif has a special charm of its own. The abrupt brown rock hills are cut through by highly fertile valleys in which the almond tree flourishes, and apricots, pomegranates and grape vines grow as well. In summer the fruit of the prickly pear is sold along the road sides, while tomatoes, sweet corn, cereals and roses are taken to the local markets.

Yet the landscape retains a wild appeal. Huge smooth boulders, strangely sculpted by wind and rain, look as though they were part of some modern landscaping venture. Brilliant blue lizards crawl across them, bats hang under the roofs of their hollowed-out interiors; some have even been converted into small homes for animals. On the remoter hillsides a flock of baboons may occasionally be spotted, the great manes of the adult males glowing in the sunshine; and foxes slink among the rocks stalking the many different birds which throng the valleys.

In this fortunate setting Taif is a town which has retained much of its traditional charm. It was known to the Prophet Muhammad who is said to have prayed in a pretty little stone mosque which stands today in the Wadi Wejj on the south-west side of the town. A few decades later, the Caliph Mu'awiya (founder of the Umayyad dynasty of Damascus) who built himself a dam, Sadd Saisid, on the north-east side of the town, remarked of a friend: 'I envy Saad as he spends spring in Jeddah, summer in Taif and winter in Mecca.'

Taif has remained a summer resort and a quarter of its total population of about 250,000 are summer residents only. It is more than just a holiday resort, however; it is also the kingdom's summer capital and the king and government move there each year in order to spend the two or three hottest months in the hills. In the mid-1970s a most original office development was completed to provide accommodation for the government during this summer period. The new offices were built inside an old Turkish barracks, the *kishla*, whose grey-brown dry-stone walls still stood intact, enclosing a large courtyard. The old rooms run along inside the external walls of the building, presenting a continuous series of arches to the interior court. The new buildings are super-modern, of white and grey concrete, yet they sit harmoniously in the old framework.

Alongside the government buildings runs one of Taif's typical wide, clean streets, lined with the delicate green *filfil* (pepper) trees which bear clusters of clear pink berries. Beside the government buildings also is one of the town's leading hotels, the Aziziya (a new Intercontinental Hotel was opened in 1977 on the road between the town and the airport), and close by the Aziziya are the narrow lanes of the old souq.

Taif has a very good souq for it is still the market town for the region. There are carpets and tents, handicrafts made by local bedouin, old guns and pistols, traditional embroidered dresses which are made in a series of tiny shops in the dress souq, gold, spices, incense and all the other attractions of an oriental market. One particularly interesting street is the old arched, brick-built military souq which still sells army uniforms and insignia. For Taif has always been and remains an important military centre with areas reserved for military training.

The old military buildings are not the only ones surviving in Taif. The town was built in the past in a style very similar to that of Jeddah and Mecca, with multi-storey family houses constructed of stone and with fine carved wooden balconies. One of the most beautiful of these houses stands on the road leading towards the airport; it was once the palace of King Faisal and is now maintained in good condition by the Ministry of Defence.

Taif was one of the first towns in the kingdom to be linked to the major cities by a network of roads. The Riyadh–Taif road was built in the early 1960s and the far more taxing Mecca–Taif road was completed in 1964. This latter road takes a direct but hazardous cliff-face route up the escarpment, which it climbs in a series of spectacular hairpin bends. It is no road for those who suffer from vertigo when looking down from great heights, but it does offer a series of magnificent views.

The Mecca–Taif road, undoubtedly the most difficult in the whole kingdom, was built before the days of great oil wealth and was designed and constructed by Saudi skills. It was built for the Ministry of Communications by the local firm of Bin Ladin; this firm was founded by Muhammad Bin Ladin, whose natural ability brought him to the attention of King Abd al Aziz (it is related that he succeeded in moving a large chandelier in the King's palace, which no one else had dared try to move).

The escarpment road was his most arduous job and one to which he devoted much of his own time, going out to sit and eat with the workmen struggling on the terrifying cliff face, solving problems of rock moving and shoring himself. The final bridge was the most difficult task and took three years to complete; it is now being rebuilt to allow more space for today's traffic and will be the highest bridge in the kingdom.

The road today can still be dangerous during storms or very heavy rainfall when it is usually temporarily closed to traffic. Fortunately such storms do not occur frequently, for they may cause rock falls which block the route. An alternative road was opened between Mecca and Taif in 1977, which takes a more gentle, northerly route through a winding valley, passing through Sayl al Kabir. This road is somewhat longer but is an all-weather route and suitable for the heaviest lorries and trailers.

It was also in 1977 that the firm of Bin Ladin, deprived by this time of its outstanding founder who had died prematurely in an air crash, but now headed by his older sons, completed construction of the road which will contribute most to opening up the fertile south west of the country. This road runs along the top of the mountain range for over 600 kilometres from Taif to Abha, passing through some beautiful scenery, especially at points where a sudden vista over the escarpment opens to the west; the builders had to cope with some difficult steep wadis here also, and large numbers of bridges,

FARMS IN THE ASIR PROVINCE

culverts and cuttings were needed.

As one drives south from Taif the scenery changes perceptibly. The sculpted rocks and cultivated valleys give way, for a while, to a barren landscape inhabited only by an occasional bedouin family, but crossed here and there by broad wadis in which it is not unusual to find flowing water. Then suddenly one meets people, for the Asir, which begins here, is one of the few regions of Saudi Arabia which is relatively densely populated. In this countryside of green terraced fields one village follows another.

Here, in the south west, one comes into a different climatic belt, a region of summer rains. Taif itself is at the very northern tip of the monsoon belt and sometimes experiences heavy storms, occasionally bringing large hailstones in midsummer. The Asir enjoys an ample rainfall of some 30 centimetres while elsewhere in the kingdom only 5 or 6 centimetres of rain falls in winter and the summers are totally dry.,

Wild flowers grow profusely in the hills and valleys of the Asir, reaching their best in March when the hillsides are scented with lavender and thyme, and one can pick handfuls of wild herbs to flavour salads and stews. The mountain tops above 2000 metres are clothed in places with fragrant juniper woods. The dense growth of these blue-berried evergreens provides shelter for a wealth of undergrowth reminiscent of an English woodland. Such woods are particularly extensive above the little town of Baha, and on the dramatic Jebel Soda, west of Abha.

The farmers of the Asir are able to raise rain-fed crops, especially along the crest of the escarpment where the rainfall is heaviest, and in the valleys where the run-off collects. Over the centuries they have constructed a patchwork of small terraced fields, retained by dry-stone walling, where in winter they sow maize, wheat and barley, giving a substantial harvest each year (including 82,000 tons of maize and 30,000 tons of wheat in one recent year). All kinds of vegetables and a quantity of fruit are also produced along with extensive crops of *berseem* (alfalfa) to feed the domestic animals.

Cultivation of these small terraced fields must often be done by draught animals and by the people themselves: the labour is intensive. Oxen pull the ploughs and donkeys carry the crops while everywhere in the fields there are people, especially women and children in brightly coloured dresses and with high-crowned, broad-brimmed straw hats. Many of the men have gone to seek their fortune in the cities, leaving their families to manage their small farms.

Today the scene in the little fields may look like a peaceful idyll of country life. In the past this was not so, judging by the large number of defensive watchtowers which are dotted among the fields, perched prominently on hill tops, or clustered in the close-built villages. These towers, into which the worker in the field must have fled in time of attack by hostile tribes, are all built to the same plan though some are far higher than others. They are entered by a low doorway near the ground while inside are a series of floors, each reached by scrambling up in the darkness through a narrow trap-door. There are no steps and one has to gain a precarious toe-hold in the dry stonework of the walls. Ascent would not have been easy with a hostile foe sitting on the floor above, waiting to clout the head of an assailant as he came up through the trap-door.

The towers stand abandoned and mostly in ruins today but many are still an attractive feature of the landscape. They are often decorated with a triangular pattern of white quartz stones running around the parapet at the top. Many are spectacularly sited, guarding a pass or a peak. Their construction follows the changing style of local architecture. In the northern Asir they are square built, of the dark brown dry-stone work of the region, and their walls curve inwards towards the top. Further south, around Abha, many of the

FARMSTEAD IN ABHA

towers are mud-built and some are circular in shape and hung with rows of tiles in the style of the houses.

These houses in the neighbourhood of Abha, capital town of the Asir, are perhaps the most picturesque and certainly the most photographed of any in the kingdom. They are tall and square, built with thick mud walls hung with horizontal rows of tiles set sloping outwards and slanting down. The rows of tiles are a metre or so apart and carry rainwater away from the walls.

The mud walls of the houses are finished with a smooth mud plaster which is painted white or cream, pale blue or pale green. In some cases a more dashing owner has painted the strips between his rows of tiles in different colours. The roofs are an important feature of these houses, and a place where the family spend much of their time. A coping, often of the crowstep crenellations which are found also in Nejd, surrounds the roof where sometimes there is a higher section fronted by a portico.

The town of Abha itself, which now has a population of about 30,000, has largely been redeveloped with modern roads, buildings and a huge dam. Its twin town of Khamis Mushayt, 27 kilometres away, and with a slightly larger population of 40,000, still partly consists of traditional buildings and has an attractive little souq which is a good source of silver jewellery. While the towns and the roads of the Asir are now largely modernized, the villages have retained their traditional aspect almost intact, set picturesquely among their vivid green terraces.

For some distance south of Khamis Mushayt one drives through a succession of villages, each more attractive than the last. Then suddenly the smiling landscape is submerged in a broken, almost lunar region of ancient lava flows, long-dead volcanoes, and sinister cinder cones. A modern road cutting reveals the original yellow sand of the district at the base of the cliff face, submerged under metres of black volcanic rock and ash.

In the midst of this daunting landscape, in the far south near the Yemen border, is a little town with a big name, Dhahran. But this is Dhahran al Janub (Dhahran of the South) and so far no oil has been found here to bring it world fame. It deserves a place in the picture books however, if not in economic histories, for it is a charming little place with lofty mud-built houses lining its main street. It offers an introduction to the tower houses of the extreme south west which are found in their full flowering in the historic valley of Najran.

The road from Dhahran turns eastwards, across a high red plain edged by flat-topped red mountains. It is a lonely land with a few semi-abandoned villages where the women dress with a satisfying sense of the total colour scheme of their environment, in green gowns and with bright yellow scarves on their heads.

Endlessly, it seems, one drives across the wide plain and then abruptly the road dips down and winds into an impressive gorge which eventually opens out, way below, into a luxuriant valley of dense palm groves. This is Najran, seat over two thousand years ago of a leading south Arabian city of that name, whose ruins are now called Ukhdud (meaning 'trenches'). The mound of the ancient city (first mentioned in the seventh century BC) stands on the southern bank of the wadi, between the water course and the abrupt, brown rock mountains which hem in and protect the valley.

In its heyday Ukhdud enjoyed a high standard of living. Well-built stone walls still stand some 3 metres above the surface of the tell, their large blocks elegantly worked with a pecked-out margin around each. On one a carving of two intertwined snakes is still visible. Although the site has not been excavated, some fine bronzes have been found there, including a fourth- or fifth-century lion's head which was for a long time on loan to the British Museum and is now exhibited in the museum in Riyadh.

The traditional buildings in the valley are of mud, not stone.

A FARM IN NAJRAN

They are grouped in a series of villages strung along the extensive wadi rather than in one large town, with bigger villages around the various markets. The houses are very high with a rather defensive air, having few and small windows on the lower floors. Each house is so large that it is the home of an extended family, and often several towers stand in one courtyard. Date palms grow close among the houses, and extensive plantations fill the space between villages.

Inside, the houses are cool and shady, their steep central staircase rising to the roof in a spiral flight of steps which slope down towards the outer edge of the tread. It is best not to descend them in a hurry, especially in the dark. The rooms are set at irregular levels, a door opening off each turn of the staircase. The walls inside are sometimes painted with scenes or geometric patterns in bright colours.

The roof is a favourite living area; mats are spread on the surface, the view is beautiful and the air fresher at that height. Meals are cooked over an open fire on a lower roof terrace, or in one of the upper rooms of the house. When we ate with Muhsin on the roof of his home in a particularly pretty little village on the wadi's edge, the mutton and rice was served on large round copper trays in the light of paraffin lanterns. We leaned on the sculpted parapet and looked across the green valley to the looming bulk of the mountains on either side, watching the sun set in a blaze of orange and red.

In the same small village we saw one of these mud tower houses being built. Stone and concrete foundations were laid, and on them the mud and straw were chopped and mixed together. A gang of men picked up balls of the mixture and passed it from one to the other, chanting rhythmically as they did so. The last man placed the firm mud pat on the wall, smoothing the sides with his hands. When a layer was complete the workers took a tea break, allowing that layer to dry before laying the next.

In the finished building the walls are curved at the corners and sweep upwards slightly at that point. The outer walls are finished with a smooth mud plaster, sometimes painted with white patterns like a cat's whiskers around the windows. Just under the roof line of larger buildings runs a fluted band of small raised half columns. The parapet itself is ornamented with decorative tracery.

Most spectacular of the buildings in Najran is the former castle of the emirs, a rambling building showing all the styles of decoration characteristic of the valley. Its square towers and round turrets with their decorative crenellations give it the appearance of a typical story-book castle, enhanced by the brightly dressed people working in the neighbouring fields.

In the valley of Najran, many people look rather like characters from a fairy tale. In the markets the men wear beautifully decorated, curved silver daggers at the front of their belts; these are the traditional *khanjar* of Arabia, though one sees them more often in antique shops today. The women are gaily dressed and many have blue tattoo marks on their chins. They are friendly and welcoming; several of the women offered our children warm milk from their goats and one nearly caused a crisis by offering a baby goat as well. A 1000-kilometre drive with a baby goat was promptly and unpopularly vetoed by the older members of the party.

6
Oil in the Eastern Province

The Eastern Province is a world of its own, like no other part of Saudi Arabia. Driving along the straight asphalt roads through the yellowish white desert, one is immediately aware that here is something different, dynamic, of huge import. This in fact is the very heart of modern Saudi Arabia, the region which has sent oil coursing through the veins of the country's economy and with it wealth beyond belief into the kingdom's coffers.

Here in the eastern deserts one feels strongly the omnipresence of oil. Pipelines snake away to the horizon; strange conglomerations of jointed valves and pipework, known in the jargon as 'Christmas trees', rear up from the sand; massive pylons carry multiple wires across the emptiness; the desert has an oddly mauled appearance – bulldozer tracks, quarries and cuttings, the signs of intense activity over the past few decades.

At evening, along the horizon, the single columns of smoke rise like sinister snakes, bent horizontal at a certain height by the prevailing wind. At night too, the gas flares which give rise to these columns reach their most dramatic moment. By day these flares show bright orange against the clear blue sky; at night they twist and whirl, orange, yellow and red, leaping four or five metres in the air and staining the great cloud of smoke above them flame-coloured by their reflection. The flames from a big flare-off create a roaring noise which drowns all conversation as one approaches them. But their day is already past; in the next few years the gas which feeds them will be collected and controlled, and there will be no more spectacular fires, no more columns of smoke along the skyline.

The curving silver pipework and great silver dome-shaped tanks of the chemical plants and refineries will multiply, however, and find echoes in the giant petro-chemical complexes to be established at Jubail on the east coast and Yanbu on the west. The oil is to be processed increasingly within Saudi Arabia from whose deserts it wells in such profusion.

The development of the oil industry has altered the whole fabric of life in Saudi Arabia more rapidly and more radically than has ever happened to any other nation in the history of mankind. Until around the middle of this century Saudi Arabia was one of the world's poorest countries, her resources limited to the annual pilgrimage, to the herds of camels and sheep which her bedouin people managed to rear on the exiguous grazing of the desert by means of a continuously nomadic existence, and to the dates and limited vegetable and cereal crops produced in the oases, and in the mountains of the south west.

Today Saudi Arabia has one of the highest *per capita* incomes in the world, thanks solely to oil. Her people are being educated, enjoying foods and clothes which their grandfathers never dreamed of, medical care, and holidays in London, Paris or New York. A successful Saudi may own a Rolls-Royce or a country manor house in England; a bedouin who has not stirred from his traditional life will own a pick-up truck and probably a water tanker as well. Both say sincerely '*Allah karim*', 'God is generous'. Many Saudis feel at heart that this sudden prosperity in some way shows that their devotion to the stricter tenets of Islam is the right course, that their people's well-being today is a justification of their faith.

This brighter future dawned for Saudi Arabia early in 1938, and that after four years of fruitless searching for oil. Today so much oil has been discovered in the kingdom that it is difficult to imagine a time when the geologists might have been wondering whether they should pack up and go home. Yet when the advance party of geologists arrived and set up camp in Jubail, in 1933, they were very optimistic. Oil had already been found on the island of Bahrain, within sight of the Saudi coast, and similar rock structures to those on Bahrain were rapidly identified near the village of Dammam. All seemed set fair for instant success.

Yet this was not to be: it was only after four years of fruitless drilling and searching that a well sunk considerably deeper than those on Bahrain finally struck oil at Dammam and the oilmen were at last in business. Standard of California had won the concession in 1933 from their British rivals, thanks to their willingness to make a down payment in gold. It was the best investment they could have made. Although the Second World War delayed the fruits of their efforts, by the end of the war they were all set for development; Standard were joined in their Saudi venture by Texaco, Standard (New Jersey) and Socony Mobil and their Saudi company was renamed the Arabian American Oil Company, known to all as Aramco.

By the end of the war the company had constructed a small refinery at Ras Tanura which came into full operation, refining 50,000 barrels a day, at the end of 1945. A submarine pipeline to

Bahrain, where much of the oil from the Saudi fields was refined, was also completed in 1945. Export of Saudi oil was already well under way but increasing world demands called for bolder measures. The journey from Ras Tanura, around the Arabian penisula and up through the Suez Canal was some 5,750 kilometres. So a pipeline, the largest crude-oil pipeline in the world, was planned to run from Abqaiq to Sidon on the Mediterranean Sea, crossing 1,700 kilometres of largely unfrequented desert.

The Trans-Arabian pipeline, known as the Tapline, was completed in 1950 and the first oil tanker was loaded at Sidon in December of that year. It was a pioneering effort in which tremendous logistic problems had to be solved. Today as one bowls along the Tapline road, running beside the pipeline across the great plain of north-east Arabia, it is difficult to remember that thirty years ago this was a trackless waste. Now modern towns with garages, petrol stations, cafès, shops and dual-carriageway main streets have been developed along the pipeline. These towns, Nu'ayriyah, Qaisumah, Hafr al Batin, Rafha abd Arar, are attracting a growing population from the desert around them. Tamarisk, oleander, eucalyptus and pepper trees have been planted along the main streets and around a few cultivated fields beside the towns. A comfortable urban life with here and there a touch of the shady green atmosphere of an old oasis is being developed there.

The oil company had already developed a new town at Dhahran, near the village of Al Khobar, for their own people. Here in their own compound the company's American employees were able to continue the home life of an American small town. Family bungalows were built along grass-lined avenues, gardens were stocked with trees and flowers. The stability of the Aramco personnel is a tribute to the success of the project: families stay in Dhahran for their whole working life, and some second-generation Americans, born and brought up in Dhahran, are working there today. A cosy, neighbourly life is led in the bungalows: T-bone steaks and angel cake form part of the evening meal, and Saudi friends dropping in feel entirely at home in this American atmosphere.

Aramco has taken great care of its employees' comfort and well-being, and in the years of development in the Eastern Province it has become almost more an institution than a company. It founded schools, hospitals and roads, encouraged local industry, sent bright young Saudis to the United States for higher education. If an employee has a problem he has only to go to the sympathetic personnel department for help: his wife does not like her bungalow – they will see about changing it; nothing grows in his garden – they provide plants; his child is sick – necessary medical attention will be arranged.

Recently Aramco has been virtually taken over by the Saudi government. The change has been smooth and amicable and although some people are anxious about the long-term results other sare confident. 'How do you feel about this?' I asked one of the American families shortly after the change was finalized. 'Oh, we're delighted,' the wife replied. 'The Saudis will look after us even better than before. They have already promised me new kitchen fittings.' In such things lies the success of keeping staff happy in a distant country with a difficult climate. The feeling that someone cares is of infinite value. And the Saudis certainly care; as one official put it, the disruption of Aramco 'could mean the disruption of the entire world economy'. They have no intention of letting that happen.

Aramco over the years has done well by doing good. The small handful of employees who landed in Jubail in 1933 has increased today to over 26,000 with a further 35,000 sub-contracted for special projects entrusted to the company by the government. Oil production, which rose to over 9 million barrels per day in 1977, was again limited to 8·5 million the following year, but there is a drive to boost production and export capacity to nearly double that figure by the end of the 1980s.

Despite this high rate of production, Aramco has every year discovered more new reserves of oil than it has extracted. Oil fields have been discovered along the shores of the Gulf, from almost as far north as the borders of Kuwait, where they are mostly offshore, to as far south as Dammam. From there the oil fields curve inland, through the large field at Abqaiq to the even larger Ghawar field. This is judged the world's biggest oil reservoir, extending for a distance of 45 by 35 kilometres. Its reserves are estimated at 68 billion barrels. West of the Ghawar field are the smaller accumulations of Khurays, Mazalij and Abu Jifan, while south-east, among the sands of the Empty Quarter, is the large proven field of Shaybah.

Today the kingdom boasts a quarter of the world's known reserves of crude petroleum, with proven reserves of some 150 billion barrels and a somewhat higher quantity of probable reserves. There are sufficient proven reserves to last at the present rate of production for about half a century, with a further half century of probable reserves. Certainly there is sufficient to keep the home fires burning for a good long time to come. They are not going to be allowed to burn at random, however. Those spectacular fires of the eastern desert are not eternal flames after all. Aramco has been commissioned to gather the gas which is at present wastefully flared and to convert it into a usable state. This $16 billion project, one of the greatest industrial undertakings of all time, will make Saudi Arabia the world's largest exporter of natural gas liquids, with a projected 650,000 barrels per day by 1985. Her gas reserves are estimated at 85,000 billion cubic feet. It will also supply the power and feedstock for the vast petro-chemical industries which are already under construction at Jubail and Yanbu.

Jubail, the fishing village where the oil geologists first landed and set up camp forty-six years ago, was a fitting choice to benefit from the end product of their labours. Yanbu, an old port on the west coast, was chosen to diversify the industrial conglomeration, to bring industry to the north west and to take advantage of a second ocean outlet. It was the more controversial of the two sites since it has to be fed by a 1,270-kilometre pipeline running across the kingdom from the oil and gas fields in the east. The increased transportation costs at this stage, however, will be offset by a shorter sea route to Europe for the finished products.

These ethylene-based petro-chemical complexes are the largest industrial developments ever undertaken. Their construction involves the development of two complete new towns and is giving Saudi planners the opportunity to try out some new ideas. They are moving away from the concept of a separate town for foreign workers, such as that at Dhahran, to an integrated housing scheme in which foreigners and Saudis will live side by side. The industries, too, will be jointly owned by the Saudi Arabian Basic Industries Corporation and foreign partners who will provide a share of the capital as well as management.

The construction of the harbour, town and petro-chemical complex of Jubail is the culmination of a continuous process of development in the Eastern Province over the past forty years. The original fishing villages of Dammam and Al Khobar have grown into flourishing towns with the new township of Dhahran forming an urban development complex with them. The three centres are still separate from each other today, but as building between them increases the gaps narrow annually. All are visibly new towns, with wide streets and modern buildings; to the east the pale turquoise waters of the Gulf extend out in endless shallows, trapping here and there a wooden dhow or fishing boat which lists sadly, waiting for the next tide to float it off. In the past these waters provided a livelihood for the townspeople; today their work is on land, at the oil wells or in trade and industry for which the oil company and its employees are the major customers.

In the past, also, the bright young men of these towns looked abroad for their education, mostly to the United States. Today the outstanding building of the region is the new University of Petroleum and Mineral Resources, crowning a rocky eminence between Dhahran and Al Khobar. This grey-white building in rough concrete, perched on its uncompromisingly irregular hillock, is one of the most satisfying new buildings in the whole kingdom. Its soaring arches cover arcades striped with light and shadow, its vistas are arranged to lead the eye to a fountain or sculpture. Its graduates are judged by independent observers to have attained the same standards as their counterparts in Britain or the United States.

In such a setting the kingdom's most promising students are preparing for a future in which they will be managing their country's most valuable economic asset, the oil industry. For it is oil alone which, over the past few years, has produced the surplus billions that have shaped the kingdom's present rapid development and have established for it a position of considerable power in the world.

7
The Sand Deserts

Two large areas of the map of Saudi Arabia are almost empty of place names. They are marked with the names 'An Nafud' and 'Ruba' al Khali' (the Empty Quarter). These are the great sand deserts, extensive areas where lofty sand dunes succeed each other like the waves of a vast yellow ocean. They fulfil the traveller's dreams of how a desert should be, but somehow rarely is.

Mapmakers attempting to depict Arabia in the past were confused by these empty areas: there must be something there, clearly their information was faulty, they decided. In an Italian map of 1599 a large lake, marked Stag Lago and fed by numerous rivers, was sited optimistically in the middle of the Empty Quarter. A later map, made in Nuremberg in 1720, filled the area with towns, villages and rivers.

One of the most fascinating aspects of Arabia today is the call of these great deserts. Where else in the world can one move out into such empty space, a land uninhabited by other people, a world of one's own. Coming from the overcrowded city life which most of us live, it is a marvellous feeling to stand alone in the desert, to look to the horizon in all directions and see no other living creature. The silence is absolute, it weighs on the ears. The sense of peace is supreme. Then, oddly, there is the excitement of spotting a distant truck, a herd of camels or bedouin camp, after days of solitude. After all, we find, we are sociable creatures. How welcoming to sit in the open black tent and chat for a while.

Such trips into the desert are our most unforgettable memories of Saudi Arabia, unique occasions which we would not have missed for anything. A desert journey is an experience which is within the range of almost everyone living in the cities of Arabia, but one which should not be undertaken lightly for it can be dangerous as well as exciting. A desert trip needs careful planning.

FAMILY RIDING A PICK-UP TRUCK

New asphalt roads extending rapidly across the kingdom have brought wide areas of desert within safe and easy reach. Anyone can drive out of Riyadh to Khulays, from Jeddah to the Mecca by-pass, from Dammam both north and west to see sand dunes a stone's throw from the road. Such outings require nothing more than a roadworthy vehicle and a bottle of drinking water, but they fail to provide that sensation of solitude which is the essence of the great desert. To find this one must strike out across the desert tracks and it is here that the risks start. Desert tracks at any distance from the asphalt roads should be undertaken only with two or more four-wheel vehicles. A shovel, matting and a tow rope should be carried in case a vehicle bogs down in sand; a tyre pump, spare petrol and large quantities of water, both for passengers and vehicles, must be included. Clothes to suit all climates are needed, for the desert can be extremely hot by day (with temperatures around 50°C) and bitterly cold at night. Some of the coldest nights I have ever spent have been in the desert, when ice stood on the water in the morning. Thick sweaters and a sleeping bag are essentials; a blanket can double to provide shade at midday or in the case of a breakdown. Always bear in mind that a breakdown can keep one in the desert for longer than planned, and stock up accordingly.

Most deserts are just barren land, gravel plains without greenery, mountains devoid of vegetation, bare earth with a few tiny plants. It is the sand deserts, however, which are the most special, for dry sand does not stay still and flat like the sand of the beach; it builds rapidly in dunes, some reaching heights of a hundred metres or so, and the dunes themselves move slowly and relentlessly across the land.

Particles of sand are carried along the ground by the wind, or they may leap in the air after collision with other sand grains. Such wind-borne sand can erode rocks like sandpaper; at Palmyra, in the Syrian desert, rows of Roman columns look as though they had been gnawed by rats a few feet above the ground – in fact they have been eroded by sand. Or the grains may meet some smaller obstacle, such as a plant, a rock, even a road sign, and collect around it. This is the start of a sand dune: in time the grains pile high, creeping up a gentle slope on the windward side, dropping down a steep slipway on the lee side, where the wind no longer carries them forward. In time the outer edges of such a dune may be carried forward on the lee side, forming the projecting horns of one of the classic crescent-shaped dunes known as a barchans.

Where the wind is constant the whole dune may gradually be moved forward, advancing in some areas as much as 30 metres a year. Such moving dunes can swamp asphalt roads, fields, even whole settlements. The ancient Roman town of Gerrha, on the Arabian Gulf, is believed to have disappeared completely beneath moving dunes.

Today intensive efforts are made to stabilize moving dunes. The first attempt to hold a large barchan dune in Saudi Arabia was made in 1963 in the Hasa oasis. The dune threatened to engulf a small town and to move on across the cultivation, but was checked by extensive irrigation and covering with plants which took root and prevented further movement. Such a solution can only be applied, however, where sufficient water is available for the plants. In the Eastern Province many dunes have been stabilized with a covering of oil. A new solution to prevent dunes forming is being tested alongside the new Riyadh–Taif highway where two-metre-wide strips of bitumenized rubber solution are laid at four-metre intervals. Sand particles blow over the strips and will not settle there.

The largest area of sand in Saudi Arabia, and indeed in the whole world, has been little touched by man. This is the forbidding

FINDING PEACE AMONG THE SAND DUNES

region of the Empty Quarter whose name, albeit somewhat deceptive, is indicative of its nature. The great dunes of the Empty Quarter, which rise in places in sand mountains up to 300 metres high, cover a region of about 650,000 square kilometres. Their yellow colour fades from a deep orange-yellow in the early morning to a whitish cream at midday.

Travellers in this region trudge up the long shallow slopes of the dunes on the windward side, their feet sinking tiringly into the sliding sand. Then they have to slither down the steep lee slopes, which sometimes produce a strange phenomenon known as the 'Singing Sands'. At times grains of sand slithering down the steep slopes can create this weird sound which has led bedouin and travellers to wonder whether the sands were haunted. Small wonder they should feel thus, for the eerie humming sound cuts oddly into the total silence of the sands.

The Al Murrah, the bedouin tribe who have made their home in the Empty Quarter, trace their ancestry back to a bedouin warrior, Murrah, who gave the tribe its name. They do not regard their homeland as 'Empty' though; to them it is simply 'The Sands', *al Rimal*. It is a homeland which they have always appreciated for its relative security from attack by others, and although they take their herds north each autumn to graze in the fairer lands of the north east, they have been happy to have the sands as a refuge to which they could retreat in case of need. Their prize herd of black camels they claim to have taken in the last century from another tribe which could not follow them back into the sands.

Food and drink were always in short supply, for everything had to be carried by the traveller, and at times became almost non-existent. A little saluki bitch, given to the explorer St John Philby as he set out, lived for days on nothing but date stones and the men in the party fared little better. Wilfred Thesiger, last of the great explorers to cross this 'bitter, dessicated land', in 1946, tells a poignant story of how, after days of fasting, they caught and cooked a desert hare. All were dreaming of how the food would taste when a group of bedouin, attracted by the smell of cooking, came to join them. Obeying the rules of desert hospitality they offered the hare to their guests and watched in an agony of hunger as the meat was eagerly devoured.

In those arid wastes traces of man's earlier presence lay undisturbed where they were left. Philby found the droppings of the camels of Bertram Thomas, his predecessor and competitor in the sands, and older camel tracks in one particularly desolate region which showed that years ago there had been rainfall and grazing there. He picked up an ostrich shell perhaps fifty years old, and a fossilized shell from several hundred thousand years ago. He found flint and bronze arrowheads and other implements, indicating that the region had been far less empty in the days of man's early existence in the peninsula.

Today the Empty Quarter is as arid as ever, but no longer so desolate or uninhabited as it was when Thomas, Philby and Thesiger made their daring journeys. 'Our next plane will be going down to the Empty Quarter on Tuesday,' says an Aramco employee. 'Why don't you come along for the day?' It is as easy as that to land in the very heart of the sands, tamed now by the ease of air travel and modern trucks, criss-crossed by scientists exploring for oil and by teams of engineers exploiting their finds. Their air-conditioned camps in hollows among the dunes are a far cry from the spartan arrangements of the travellers of thirty or forty years ago.

Rivalling the Empty Quarter in appearance if not in size, is the sand desert of the great Nafud, in the north. Here rolling red sand dunes cover an area of some 60,000 square kilometres; their colour, which appears as a deep orange-red in the early morning and at evening, is caused by strains of iron oxide in the

MEN AROUND A CAMP FIRE

sand. This reddish colour is warmer, somehow more welcoming, than the yellow dunes of the south, and in the Nafud it is offset by the grey-green of tamarisk bushes growing here and there in the hollows.

The Nafud has never held quite the mystery of the Empty Quarter. It is frequented by bedouin in winter and spring, and was early crossed by western travellers. Palgrave, the first of these, described the Nafud in 1862 as 'an immense ocean of loose reddish sand'. He was also the first to remark on strange deep hollows among the dunes, which reminded him of Edgar Allan Poe's 'Maelstrom', and which were so steep that he had difficulty descending to the bare chalky ground at their base.

The hollows, known as *fulj,* were described in greater detail by Lady Anne Blunt who crossed the Nafud with her husband in search of Arabian horses in 1878. She estimated that the horsehoof-shaped depressions covered from one acre to two hundred acres, and their diameter was often at least a quarter of a mile. Her husband concluded that they must be the result of some hollowing action of the wind.

Long fingers of dune terrain stretch southwards from the Nafud, through central Nejd past Buraydah and Unayzah, and south-eastwards in the form of the Dahna to merge eventually into the

Empty Quarter. Some of these narrower sand deserts are especially beautiful, cradling palm groves in the hollows between dunes, and supporting quite a range of desert bushes whose green foliage blends harmoniously against the red background.

It is unexpected, at first sight, to find plants growing successfully in what appear to be totally arid wastes, yet virtually all the desert of Saudi Arabia (with the exception of some regions in the heart of the Empty Quarter) supports plant life. These plants are specially adapted to survive with a minimum of water, having long root systems, small thin leaves which lose little moisture from transpiration, or thick fleshy cactus-type foliage which retains moisture. Their seeds lie dormant in the desert for years, springing into life and flowering only after a rainfall. Some bushes, such as the scarlet-fruited *abal,* are said to be able to survive for four years after one shower of rain. In spring, after rain, the whole desert to the horizon may acquire a green sheen, looking at first sight like luscious turf. On closer inspection the green consists of minute plants, set somewhat sparsely, which soon bear tiny but beautiful flowers.

The animals and reptiles which live on these plants (or on each other) are also specially adapted to life in a harsh environment; they can live with little or no water, many being nocturnal and thus avoiding desiccation in the sun. Most of the animals are sandy coloured, for camouflage in the desert, and run extremely fast, their only means of escaping predators. Many of the larger birds and animals of the desert, such as the oryx, gazelle and ostrich, have become extinct or virtually so in this century since flight, their traditional means of defence, was to no avail against hunters in motor vehicles equipped with guns. Today these animals are protected and hunting them is illegal, but it is already too late to save the oryx and ostrich in their natural habitat, and the gazelle is now rarely sighted.

The bedouin, the desert's other hardy inhabitants, might have suffered the same fate had not King Abd al Aziz put a stop to their warfare and raiding in the 1930s and 1940s. In the past century bedouin armed with lances and mounted on camels could only inflict limited damage on their foes. In the early decades of this century the widespread possession of rifles and the introduction of cars to desert warfare greatly increased their scope for killing. The number of dead in desert battles reached serious proportions.

King Abd al Aziz saw the dangers of this and insisted that peace in the desert was essential to the creation of a stable state. He was the first ruler for centuries to be able to enforce his will on the bedouin tribes, who respected their powerful desert leader and became his most devoted subjects. Many of them also complied

AGRICULTURE AMONG THE ANCIENT RUINS OF AL JAWF

with his wish that they should abandon their nomadic life and settle on the land.

Over the past few decades large numbers of the bedouin have settled in the oases and cities, and many more have become only semi-nomadic. Hamad of the Harb tribe is an example. He lives in a hut on the outskirts of Jeddah and grazes his camels for most of the year along the sea coast just beyond the building works. He is very pleased with his little house which he regards as distinctly superior to a tent. In spring he takes his camels up to the mountains to fatten them for selling at pilgrimage time, and only then does he lead a truly nomadic life. His children go to school in Jeddah and are likely to have city jobs when they leave school. And so another family will have left the desert.

For the 600,000 bedouin who have stayed as nomads, the changes have also been great. Many families have abandoned herding camels.

These well-adapted desert animals had enabled them to go into the inner deserts, provided milk, meat and wool, as well as serving as riding animals and beasts of burden. Today sheep are more profitable and grazing can be provided for them thanks to motor transport. Every tent now seems to be equipped with a four-wheel-drive pick-up truck and these hardy little vehicles give their owners immense flexibility. They can be loaded with empty oil cans which are filled with water to save men and animals from the constant dangers of drought which haunted them in the past; or they bring in large loads of firewood for cooking and to keep the family warm. The sheep, and even a few camels, can be loaded in the back and taken off to find better pastures or to market. When the whole family moves, the tent, belongings, children and dogs are piled in the back and a long journey rapidly made. Muhsin of the Rwala comes down from Jordan into northern Saudi Arabia with his family and flocks in autumn, making the journey each year by pick-up. When he was a child it used to take them days on camel back. No, he would not like to go back to those times.

Many camps supplement their pick-up with a water tanker, or a large truck in which the whole herd can be moved to new grazing. In the last few years the entire desert has become crisis-crossed by a spider's web of tracks running in every direction; not infrequently one follows a well-worn track only to find that it peters out at some abandoned camp site. Today such a site might be marked by empty sardine and milk-powder tins, a punctured oil drum and a split truck tyre, as well as by the traditional stones of the coffee fire and piles of camel dung. New foods and new implements have been readily taken into the tents. Why risk the children running short of milk when milk powder is as efficient as the camels; why live on rice and bread when sardines and tomato paste add so much more flavour to meals? Why hunt all day for the right track when a compass will set you staight in a moment, or for a lost sheep when a pair of binoculars lengthens the eyesight marvellously?

The bedouin are proving very adaptable, both in their willingness to settle to city life, and in their acceptance of new ways in the desert. They are still the only people who can make use of over ninety per cent of the land of Saudi Arabia, and their contribution to the kingdom's needs for meat and animal products is substantial. Their time-honoured skills still play a useful role in the modern economy, thanks to the help which they get from the government in the purchase of equipment and in times of hardship. Their hospitable tents are still open to the desert traveller; without them the desert would really become a dead land.

8
Arts and Crafts of Arabia

Arabia's greatest cultural offering must be the Arabic language. Immensely rich and flexible, forged in the towns and deserts of the sparsely populated Arabian peninsula, it is today spoken by over 120 million people. It is the national language of all the Arab countries, from Oman in the east to Morocco in the west, and is understood by many non-Arab Muslims as well, for it is the language of the Quran.

Arabic is considered one of the world's difficult languages. This is not because it is illogical or unpredictable in its structure; on the contrary, the grammar is beautifully clear and a range of prefixes and suffixes enables the speaker to construct large numbers of words with predictable meanings from a basic root word of three consonants. The difficulty with Arabic lies in its richness. Its wealth of vocabulary gives the speaker a choice of words for any given object or concept, and the choice is often not the one which the foreign student happens to have learnt.

Since early times, Arabic has been written in an attractive alphabetic script. The alphabet which we, the Arabs and most other peoples in the world use today, was developed in and near the Arabian peninsula. It was first invented by the Canaanites and their successors, the Phoenicians, and rapidly adopted by the early Arabian kingdoms. Different peoples gradually wrote the letter signs differently, some writing from left to right as we do, some from right to left in the Arab fashion. However the Latin and Arabic alphabets are still sufficiently similar to show their common origin.

For the Arabs their written language was to become an art form in its own right. Many beautifully carved rock inscriptions exist throughout Arabia from pre-Islamic times. After the spread of Islam inscriptions – usually incorporating a Quranic text – became a favourite style of decorative art. They were carved, sculpted or painted on the walls of buildings, glazed onto tiles or pottery, illuminated in manuscripts.

Elegant forms of writing were developed: the angular Kufic was the earliest of these, followed by the more cursive Naskhi. One of the earliest examples of the Kufic script is the inscription carved in 58 AH (680 AD) on the Sadd Saisid dam near Taif in the Hejaz. In later decorative panels formed with Arabic script, the lettering became at times so ornate that it was difficult to read at all. The meaning behind the ornamentation was always there, however, and its purpose, to praise God, remained paramount.

A quite different, secular use of Arabic in the rich poetry of the desert, was well developed in the century before Islam. These traditional poems display the full wealth of the language and the versatile skill of the poet, and the style has remained popular to the present day. Poetry has the advantage that it can easily be learned by heart. It has, therefore, always been especially appropriate for nomadic peoples who can take little baggage with them and must carry their history and folklore in their heads.

The poems of ancient Arabia are long and narrative odes. They tell of desert life, of love and war, and their images are drawn from the scenes of the desert, the animals and landscape and the brilliant stars of the night sky. The rhyme scheme is an essential part of the poem, the same rhyme being kept up throughout and involving the last two or even three syllables of every line. The poet's skill lay not in producing new subjects and styles but in finding ever richer images and rhyme schemes.

Poetry is still Saudi Arabia's favourite art form; it is the subject of public declamations and private writing. Poems are composed and recited for weddings and festivals, poetic games are played at such gatherings where each man in turn must contribute a line to a corporate poem, until he can follow the rhyme scheme no longer.

Rhythm is also an important feature of Arabic poems which are often sung rather than recited. They might be accompanied by a lute, the single-stringed *rababa*, the simple instrument of both desert and town, or the round-bellied, five-stringed *'aud*. Sometimes a small drum or tambourine accompanies the singer as well. The stretched skin, of which drum, tambourine and *rababa* are constructed, can be tightened for playing by heating before an open fire. Arabic poetry and music seem at their most evocative in the setting of a camp fire at night although today more people probably hear them over the radio and television.

As the musicians sat around their fire in the past the firelight would have reflected on their silver daggers and powder casks, on the brass and copper coffee pots by the hearth, and on the silver bracelets, necklaces and head ornaments worn by the women. This

THE ANTIQUE SOUQ IN RIYADH

metalwork was always an important craft in Arabia and continues to be so today, though now the favourite metal is gold rather then silver or copper.

The richest sights of today's cities are the gold souqs where the small stalls display such a glittering array of gold chains, pendants, rings and bracelets that it is hard to believe they are real, especially at night when they glint under the naked electric light bulbs. The gold souq is always packed with women shoppers bargaining to get

THE WOMEN'S SOUQ IN RIYADH

the best price for objects which are, however, sold more by the weight than the workmanship. Not all the shoppers are rich; gold is thought a good investment in desert and town and has replaced silver as the chosen jewellery of the bedouin. Two charming bedouin women offered us a gold ring each when we visited their tent; when we tried to refuse they insisted: 'Take them. It is nothing. Just a small souvenir of the pleasant time we have spent together.'

The silver stalls in the souqs are now more frequented by foreigners than by Saudis. 'Bedouin silver' is acquiring an antiquity value and each year there are fewer stalls and fewer pieces for sale. Most of the silver in the souq is old and well worn; sometimes it is renovated by 'dipping'. Although the silverwork is often described as 'bedouin jewellery', it was not in fact made by the bedouin. It was the work of craftsmen in the towns and oases but was always popular with the bedouin whose taste it must sometimes have reflected. Sophisticated techniques of metalwork, such as filigree and granulation (the soldering of droplets onto a background), were often used, but so too were quite primitive methods such as setting a coloured stone in place with date paste.

Silver was frequently obtained by melting down Maria Theresa dollars, the universal coin of the peninsula in centuries past. This was combined with some other suitable metal, such as copper, to produce jewellery with a rather low silver content. Semi-precious stones and small coins were often built into a piece of jewellery, amber, coral and turquoise being especially popular though glass beads and cowrie shells were also used. Many necklaces had a protective as well as a decorative function, consisting as they did of a small oval or oblong casket in which a verse of the Quran could be placed.

Men did not wear jewellery as the women did but their weaponry was often beautifully ornamented and some of the finest silverwork is found on the sheaths of daggers from the past. The daggers might be the broad, curved *khanjars* or the slender, almost straight daggers which could be long or short. Their sheaths were decorated with plaited silver threads, filigree work, combinations of gold and silver. Today they are much in demand by collectors and prices for fine ones are high.

Some of the powder casks worn by men at the belt or on a shoulder strap were also very ornate, of incised silverwork or wrought in the form of a curved horn. They accompanied long flintlock rifles which might be equally decorative, set with silver plate along the barrel or on the stock. A more simple form of decoration, but one much favoured by huntsmen in the past century, was to stick on the butt the teeth of the gazelle or oryx which they had shot, and to pad the end of the butt with gazelle hide.

Hand-wrought metalwork produced many of the simpler items of everyday use in the past. Foremost among these, in a land which has raised hospitality to a veritable art, was the coffee pot and all the

A MUDHOUSE KITCHEN

equipment which went with the process of coffee making. Coffee pots are made in regional styles, some of which are very ornate with incised patterning. They are of copper or brass and vary in size from huge ornamental pieces made for the palace of a prince, to the small, homely brass pots still produced in quantities today. A row of coffee pots was the essential feature of the guest hearth of any bedouin tent, village cottage or palace majlis. Coffee is still served to guests from such pots today, poured with dexterity into tiny cups from a considerable height.

Along with the coffee pots went the pestle and mortar, of brass, stone or wood, in which the freshly roasted beans were ground. The ring of pestle on mortar drew guests to the coffee hearth just as a lunch bell brings schoolboys hurrying in, or calls workers from the factory floor. The coffee beans were roasted before grinding in a pan with a long ornate handle and stirred with a matching, long-handled stirrer. These decorative sets of skillet and stirrer can still be found in the antiques souqs, along with the little wooden dishes in which the beans were placed to cool.

Metalwork was often combined with woodwork in the household implements of the past. The coffee cooling dishes, wooden milking bowls and wooden chests might be decorated with brass or white metal studs; large chests were sometimes virtually covered with incised thin plate brass and studs. Such objects were treasured and used for many years: most of the bowls have been mended, some several times over, with leather stitching or wire clips.

Wood was always scarce in Arabia but it was used for many purposes and wooden objects are often ornate. In the villages and towns of central Arabia the doors of rooms and cupboards were decorated with incised geometric patterns and painted in bright colours – blues, greens, yellows, browns and reds. Well wheels, over which the rope ran to the well bucket, were often treated in the same way, their spokes painted in patterns of red and brown.

Centuries ago the bedouin developed the wooden 'tree' for their camel saddles, an elongated triangle of crossed pieces of wood, fitting over the camel's hump and distributing the weight of rider or baggage onto his rib cage. These saddle trees are often decorated with incised patterns and their pommels sometimes inlaid with silver. They served a double purpose: when not on the camel's back they were set beside the coffee hearth and covered with sheep skins or rugs, as pieces of furniture against which the men reclined. They are still used for this purpose today, in the tents of bedouin who may not have kept camels for many years.

More ornate than the saddle trees were the wooden litters in which women and children rode when the camp was on the move. They were made of curved branches of wood, the style varying from tribe to tribe. When in use they were draped with gaily coloured pieces of cloth, giving them the appearance of great butterflies swaying across the desert. Such litters are rarely used today, for the families travel faster and more comfortably by truck, but they and the saddle trees can sometimes be found in the antiques souq of Riyadh.

The most sophisticated and ornate examples of Arabia's woodwork, and the most prolific, are found in the old houses of the Western Province, in Jeddah, Mecca, Taif and Yanbu. These houses were closed by heavy wooden doors, ornamented with relief carvings of leaves, flowers and fruit. Similar panels were often set below the windows which were enclosed with wooden casements or balconies, projecting out from the wall of the house and piled one above the other, three or four storeys high. Rows of wooden stalactites hung from the hoods above the balconies, and from their bases; fretted trellis-work panels made up the main structure. This high-quality work was done by Arabian carpenters using wood imported from Africa and the East. Teak was most popular since it withstood the rigours of sun and salty breeze.

Such woodwork is no longer undertaken today but in recent years a new popular art form has appeared in the painted wood panels which decorate most of the large trucks plying across the country. These trucks are painted a bright background colour, orange, green or blue, and their superstructure is decorated with geometric patterns. The lower sections are painted with scenes of lakes, sailing boats and houses with pointed roofs, looking for all the world like a Dutch landscape; or they may show flowers, birds or occasionally animals. The panels are painted in small workshops in the towns, to the truckdrivers' choice of design. This truck art is oddly reminiscent of the barge art which flourished on the canals of Europe during the past century.

Almost as colourful as the trucks, though in a quite different way, are the goods produced by the ancient craft of weaving. Weaving is Arabia's most traditional and basic craft, for it is on the loom that the women have always produced the strips of cloth from which their black tents are made. The loom they use is a long, narrow one which is stretched out on the ground, the threads held in place by a cross pole at either end. The women sit on the floor to weave, pressing each row of wool into place with little picks made of gazelle horns. The work is heavy and strength and skill are needed to produce the close-woven, watertight sections of a tent.

The black or black-and-white-striped tent sections are enlivened by brightly coloured dividing curtains, rugs, bags and camel trappings which are also made on the loom. These are decorated with geometric patterns, often made up of triangles, and woven in a variety of strong colours. In the past these colours were made with natural dyes, giving predominantly yellows, reds and browns. Today the wool is dyed with chemical dyes in the towns and new colours such as oranges, purples and greens are available. The skeins of coloured wools can sometimes be seen hanging to dry against the walls of the souqs by the dye vats.

Weaving is practised rather less than it used to be but the colourful bags and rugs still find a good market in the towns. In the Eastern Province an enterprising young Saudi woman has recently

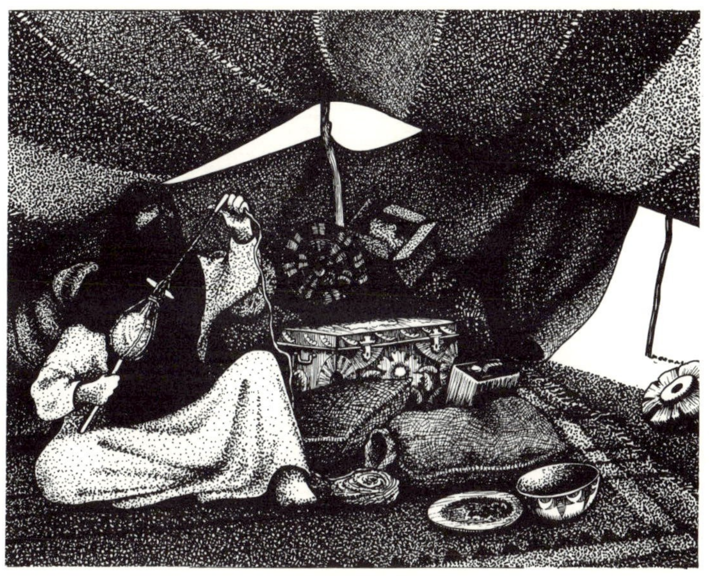

A BEDOUIN WOMAN SPINNING

been encouraging the country women to weave goods with a modern appeal, and has helped them market the produce. In the Community Centres, such as the one at Diriyah, village women are also encouraged to weave, being provided with a shed in which to work and with an outlet for their wares through the permanent exhibition of hand-crafts on display there.

Besides woven goods, made from the wool of their flocks which is spun as they sit guarding their animals, the women have also always made some leather goods from the hides. These are worked into storage bags, today mostly of small size for the large water bags are now made from truck tyres and inner tubes. Small leather bags are used to store grain, sugar and coffee; they are decorated with fringes and tassels, burnt patterns, and a whole range of colourful effects made possible by the materials now available in the souq. In some tents near Taif the women brought out traditional bags with leather fringes but quickly pushed these aside to display their best handwork, leather bags embroidered with coloured silks and encrusted with buttons and small beads and finished at the neck with cyclamen-coloured nylon. The bright colours of this mixture of old and new materials clearly delighted them and commanded four times the price of the traditional bags in the souq, they said.

9
Arabia in Antiquity

Those who travel into the arid inner deserts of Saudi Arabia soon become aware that they are not the first people to visit these remote regions, even though the initial impression is strong that no others could ever have trodden that way. The observant traveller begins to notice that not all the stones are as nature left them, that some in fact must have been worked by man.

Strangest perhaps of the irregular desert rocks is the large collection found some 74 kilometres north-east of Riyadh. Here a totally barren stretch of desert is littered with chunks of rock, some of enormous size, which look for all the world like pieces of wood, branches or trunks of trees. Yet when one tries to lift them one finds that they do not only feel like rock, they also weigh as heavily as rock.

These are in fact the fossilized remains of a forest which once flourished beside an inland lagoon here. They are thought to be between 65 and 100 million years old and to include the remains of date palms as well as of several deciduous species of trees. These pieces of fossilized wood illustrate, perhaps more graphically than any other remains in the desert, just how much the climate of Arabia has changed over the ages.

The fossil wood is found only in a few places, but prehistoric flint tools, left lying on the desert surface where their Stone Age users dropped them, are found throughout the kingdom. 'After a while you get a feel for the places that appealed to the Stone Age hunters. You look for a sheltered spot, a good source of flint, perhaps a wadi nearby,' remarked one seasoned desert traveller. In such places one may often find a flint working site, a litter of chips and flakes and the central core from which they were struck. There may be a few broken flint tools, the 'rejects' of the flint knapper's product, occasionally a perfect arrow-head or blade.

A rich collection of these flint tools, beginning with palaeolithic implements, and continuing through mesolithic and neolithic times, is on display in the new archaeological museum in Riyadh. The museum offers the best opportunity to learn about these tools and to admire the wide range of implements produced in Arabia. But there is nothing to compare with the sudden excitement of coming across such a flint tool in the desert, of knowing that it was last held by human hand some 20,000 years ago.

Many of the later flints were made by master craftsmen and in the Arabian desert suitably hard stone of many colours was available. The small, shiny arrow-heads especially are works of art and have sometimes been converted into pieces of jewellery, mounted in a gold clasp. They were made as weapons but the men who made them were also artists. This artistic talent was put to good use in ancient Arabia in the large numbers of rock carvings which exist throughout the peninsula and which in many places have survived in a perfect state of preservation. The pictures were made by hammering on a cliff face with a hard stone, and then by polishing to produce a smooth, engraved surface to the design.

Most of these ancient pictures show the animals which the artists herded and domesticated, or those which they hunted. There are pictures of dogs with pointed ears and curled-up tails, just like the desert pie-dogs of today. There are ibex and gazelle too, but no camels at all in these earliest carvings.

Most unexpected, and perhaps most characteristic of these friezes, are the herds of long-horned cattle portrayed. These cattle have flat backs (unlike the humped zebu cattle of Arabia today). They are found now in the Sudan and along the southern fringes of the Sahara but could no longer survive in the arid conditions of the Saudi desert. It is these cattle pictures rather than any others which have helped to indicate the date of the rock carvings. The absence of camels in the early carvings shows that they were fashioned perhaps before 1000 BC. The presence of cattle shows that they were made not later than around 3000 BC when desiccation had really gripped the deserts.

A perfect example of Arabian prehistoric carvings is to be seen on the great rock of Hanakiya, 30 kilometres east of the village of that name and 120 kilometres east of Medina along the road towards Qasim. The large red-rock outcrop, just to the north of the main road, has almost vertical cliff faces on which several friezes of animals were carved in ancient times, along with numerous individual specimens. The largest frieze shows cattle with immensely long horns, depicted with their heads turned sideways, as though the horns were viewed from above. On the beasts' flanks are strange

ANCIENT GRAFFITI AT JEBEL AJA, SOUTH EAST OF HAIL

patches – were they piebald or did they wear some kind of trappings? Similar patches are drawn on such cattle pictures elsewhere in Arabia and as far west across the Sahara as Morocco.

The cattle are herded, in this frieze, by men wearing short tunics and with their hair tied back in a pony tail. These men are helped by little dogs. Even stranger human figures are shown in a lively rock carving in the Sakaka oasis, on the Jebel Burnus, a rocky outcrop projecting from the near-vertical rock which is crowned by the Zabal fort. Here a group of figures, dressed also in short tunics, are shown apparently dancing, each one waving his arms in the air. On their heads they all wear what looks like a great comb but must surely have been some fringed or feathered headdress.

Other rather different carvings on these rocks and elsewhere show camels, donkeys, and bedouin on horseback waving long lances. Where such pictures occur near those of the cattle the difference is clear: they are far lighter in colour, not having had time to acquire the dark patina of age, and they have been picked out but not polished. The bedouin artists had less time for their sculpture than the herdsmen of ages past.

Those herdsmen, or their bedouin successors, may have left

another sign of their activity in the huge stone circles which mark the deserts from north to south of Arabia. From the ground these circles are not easy to spot, but if one flies over the desert at not too high an altitude, one is struck by the great numbers of circles and the strange straight walls which run from them at a tangent.

Some of these circles, which range in diameter from 20 to 100 metres, have reasonably high walls, and may indeed have been used for herding animals which could have been driven in along the straight sides. Others, however, stand only a few stones high and could hardly have restrained even a baby calf or camel. Their purpose remains a mystery: some seem to have been cemeteries for they enclose stone-built grave mounds; others may have indicated the presence of water, for their shape exactly coincides with the old Himyaritic sign for water – a line projecting from a circle. Such signs were certainly carved on rocks; it is possible that they might have been built in the desert also for in many cases the straight wall appears to point directly to a water source.

The rock-built grave mounds which are sometimes sited within the large circles, or along the lines of walls, are far from being the only ancient burial mounds in Arabia. In the Eastern Province in particular there are thousands of these mounds, similar in appearance to those on the island of Bahrain, many of which are known to be nearly 5000 years old. These mounds often consist of a burial chamber built of stone and then covered with a large pile of earth.

In the Eastern Province numerous traces have been found of one of the world's earliest civilizations, that which is known from the site of Al Ubaid in Iraq where it was first identified. Distinctive pottery, shells, flint implements and building plaster have been found at many sites along the eastern seaboard and running inland towards the Empty Quarter beside a great depression, once an arm of the sea. In these ancient coastal villages, which were inhabited some 6000 to 7000 years ago, the people seem to have lived in plastered reed-built houses similar to those of the Marsh Arabs of Iraq today.

While these Al Ubaid sites consist of such low tells that few people would spot them, the island of Tarut just off the east coast boasts a spectacular, huge tell crowned by the ruins of a Portuguese fort. The tell consists of the remains of a town which lasted from the third to the first millenium BC and was closely related to the ancient culture of Dilmun, discovered on Bahrain island in a very similar tell.

The tell on Tarut island has not been excavated but development work on the island in the 1960s led to the discovery of many finely

SPICE MERCHANT

carved black steatite vases and a large Sumerian-style stone statue, now on display in the museum in Riyadh. Tarut may once have been a major city in the ancient kingdom of Dilmun, and a leading trading port with the city states of ancient Mesopotamia, with Uruk, Ur, Babylon and Nineveh.

Eastern Arabia boasted another great trading city in ancient times: the city of Gerrha. Gerrha flourished in the last few centuries before Christ and the first century AD. Its inhabitants traded spices and incense with Greece and Rome and grew rich on their trade. Their city was five miles in circumference, according to Pliny; Strabo, writing a little earlier, described the 'costly magnificence of their houses' whose 'doors, walls, and roofs are variegated with inlaid ivory, gold, silver and precious stones'. Many people in recent times have sought for the remains of this once wealthy city, but without success. Gerrha seems to have disappeared without trace, possibly beneath advancing sand dunes.

The incense and spices on which Gerrha's prosperity was based,

NABATAEAN TOMBS AT MEDAIN SALIH

were brought overland across Arabia from the incense lands of the south west, Arabia Felix. The caravan route passed through the inland city of Fau, on the edge of the Empty Quarter, and at the foot of the Tuwayq escarpment. This city, though less famous than Gerrha in ancient times, is better known today thanks to excavations carried out there by Riyadh University. It flourished in the fourth and third centuries BC and some fine Hellenistic objects have been discovered in its ruins.

The caravan trade across Arabia flourished for many centuries, throughout the first millenium BC and on into our era. Frankincense, which grew in the highlands of southern Yemen and Dhofar, was much in demand in the wealthy lands of the Mediterranean, Egypt, Greece and Rome. Incense has always been appreciated as a perfume and in religious ritual; it was especially in demand in funeral rites until it went out of use with the spread of Christianity, and the rich trade came to an end.

During the heyday of the incense trade the caravan trails saw a lively traffic carried by strings of camels whose domestication had made the trade possible. Their passage is recorded in the hundreds of thousands of inscriptions carved into the rocks of Arabia by caravan men, at a time when northern Europe was still totally illiterate.

One of the most ancient of these caravan routes ran through Mecca and Medina. North of Medina the track picked its way through the mountains of the Hejaz to the oasis of Al Ula, mentioned in the Bible by its ancient name of Dedan. Today the attractive mud town of Al Ula is strung along a sandy valley, surrounded by its orange orchards and palm groves, and hemmed in by cliffs of red sandstone. Inscriptions have been carved into these cliffs in many ancient Arabian tongues, and north-east of the city a row of square openings has been cut into the cliffs, like a series of glassless windows. A pair of lions carved above some of the openings are the only ornament to this otherwise bare cliff face. But these simple tombs served as a prelude to the far more decorative rock-cut tombs of Medain Salih, 15 kilometres further north.

The Nabataeans, an Arab tribe of the Hejaz who had made their capital at Petra, in what is now Jordan, gained control of the northern caravan trade in the centuries before Christ. By the first century BC their influence extended south as far as Dedan and they built a colony of their own at Hijra (now known as Medain Salih), just to the north of it. They had an eye for a beautiful site: Medain Salih, though quite different in atmosphere from Petra, certainly rivals that famous 'rose-red city' in picturesque appeal. The rock cliffs are golden, eroded in places into strange mushroom shapes, and rising from a bed of clean gold sand. It is an open, sunny place, with none of the air of foreboding which still hangs over Petra (of which the Bible prophesied that 'thorns shall come up in her palaces, nettles and brambles in the fortresses thereof . . . (and) there shall the vultures also be gathered . . .').

In the course of a century the Nabataeans carved over a hundred tomb chambers with sculptured façades in the rock cliffs at Medain

Salih. The chambers were designed to serve a whole family as their final resting place. Although their great doorways now gape empty they must once have been closed with wooden doors (traces of bolt holes are occasionally visible in the jambs) while inside loculi, like shelves, were cut in the rock as and when needed, or large walk-in niches were constructed to take shelves on which many family members could be laid.

Above the doors, the businesslike folk of Medain Salih carved inscriptions giving the names of the owners, the date of construction, and the name of the mason; they called down the wrath of the gods on whosoever should violate their tombs, and imposed a Nabataean fine of, say, 1000 drachmas as well. Inscriptions of this kind are rare at Petra but at Medain Salih they are the rule rather than the exception. They date the tombs to the years between 1 BC and 76 AD. The script is of particular interest, for from it developed Kufic and from that, ultimately, modern Arabic.

The tomb façades of Medain Salih show the same Nabataean architectural styles as those of Petra: the pilasters with their simple capitals on either side of the doorway, the crowstep decoration above the cornice, the sculpted eagles and urns. Many of the latter have been damaged in the past by bedouin shooting at them in an attempt to obtain the treasure which they supposed them to contain. On our way there we were invited to tea in a tent and our hosts urged us to let them help us recover the treasure whose whereabouts, they were certain, we must know, else why should we visit such a place?

The tombs of Medain Salih lack the grandeur of the larger tombs at Petra and are more homogeneous in style; the Roman extravaganzas such as the Palace Tomb of Petra are missing here. But these more characteristically Nabataean structures are also, by and large, much better preserved than those of Petra; they thus produce a more cheerful impression.

A new road has recently been built almost to Al Ula, which branches off the main Medina–Tobuk highway a little to the north of Khaybar. This road is being extended westwards to Al Wejh and there are plans to continue the road system north through Medain Salih, along the old caravan route to Tobuk. It is already relatively easy to visit Medain Salih (about 400 kilometres by road from Medina) since only the last 20 kilometres remains as track. Permission from the Ministry of the Interior to visit the site must however be obtained first.

A new archaeological museum was opened in Riyadh in 1977, in which objects found throughout the kingdom are displayed. The

NABATAEAN TOMB IN MEDAIN SALIH

museum, which aims to play a teaching role, is in the premises of the Department of Antiquities in Imam Abd al Aziz ibn Muhammad Street. The objects are beautifully displayed and their origin and purpose fully explained by means of wall panels, photographs, slide projections and other audio-visual aids. Future plans for the development of the kingdom's archaeology include museums at the major sites, regional museums, and a national museum housed in the large Murabba Palace in Riyadh. An archaeological survey of the whole kingdom is now being undertaken by the Department of Antiquities with the assistance of experts from abroad.

10
Oases in the Desert

Arabia is not today, nor ever has been, entirely a desert inhabited purely by nomadic herdsmen. Although, looking down from an aeroplane flying across those endless wastes of tawny brown, one may have the impression that Arabia is nothing but sand, this is not in fact the case. Here and there the brown is punctuated by a splash of green – an oasis. These oases have played a role in the country's history which has been quite disproportionate to their size.

An oasis can only be established where there is a perennial source of water, usually in a wadi or beside a permanent spring. Where there is reliable water of this kind today there was also water in the past, even in very ancient times. At such sites villages or small towns were built, often thousands of years ago. Many of the oases of northern Saudi Arabia are listed in that most ancient of sources, the Book of Genesis; many are also mentioned in the records of the aggressive ancient Assyrians as sites which were besieged, plundered or forced to pay tribute. These records take us back some 3000 years in the history of oases which were clearly already well known to the neighbouring states at that time.

These little towns, rather than the nomadic tribes of the desert, attracted the covetous eyes of neighbours. Here the wealth of the country was concentrated, here a cultured life developed; from here influence was exerted. By the seventh century AD the most flourishing oases were those along the caravan routes, and notably Mecca and Medina. These two oases were to play a decisive role in the history of the world, for here the Prophet Muhammad was born and lived his life, and from here the religion of Islam was preached to mankind. The events which took place in the two small oasis towns in the early part of the seventh century altered the life of a vast region of the world and of millions of people far beyond the borders of the Islamic lands.

A civilized life continued over the centuries in many of the oases.

OASIS TOWN

When Charles Doughty visited the oasis of Al Ula in the Hejaz, a century ago, he was offered coffee, sweet lemons and splendid dates which the townspeople exported to Damascus. 'There is no more civil life than theirs, even at Damascus,' he commented, and added: 'I wondered to see this people of Quran readers, bred up in a solitary valley of desolate mountains amidst immense deserts, of that quiet behaviour and civil understanding. The most of the men are lettered.'

Nevertheless this comfortable life carried its risks. The oases, as Doughty had remarked, were isolated in the wilderness. They had to look to their own defence for no one else could help them. In Al Ula, as he saw, the townsmen always went armed in their own streets. In many of the oases strong fortresses were built on outcrops of rock;

some were surrounded by great walls, and most built watchtowers as outposts on the surrounding hills. Many oases established links with a local bedouin tribe who would defend them, and who may indeed have made their headquarters in the oasis town.

Today the peace established by King Abd al Aziz covers the land. The oases are being progressively linked not only to one another but also to the major communications systems of the kingdom, by new asphalt roads. There is no longer any call for defence and the fortresses are largely in ruins, the circuit walls crumbling and the watchtowers falling down. No one goes armed in the oases today; their lifeline to the outside world is assured by radio, telephone and the petrol stations which have sprung up along the main street.

In the little grocery shops which now invariably accompany the petrol stations one can buy tinned fruit juice from Japan (suitably chilled in the refrigerators of course), tinned peaches from America and tinned cream from Denmark. Fresh dates might be harder to find, but there are plenty of oranges, apples and bananas.

In the past, however, dates were the staple food of the oases and the date palm was, literally, their staff of life. This tolerant tree will flourish where there is very little water – hence its great value in Arabia – and also where the soil has become saline through centuries of irrigation, hence its value in the oases. It is the oasis tree par excellence, the one without which all other oasis cultivation would come to an end, for the fruit trees, vegetables, alfalfa and other plants are all grown in its shade. Its great value has always been recognized and respected by the Arabs, in whose lands it may have originated. Ancient Sumerian legend placed the origin of the date palm in Dilmun, which was most probably a state comprising the island of Bahrain and the neighbouring Saudi coast, including the ancient city on the island of Tarut.

The date palm was not only a prime source of nourishment, it was also an important building material. The palm trunks served as rafters and posts (this may have been the origin of the concept of the column as an architectural feature) and the branches for roofing. The triangular pattern, points down, which is so popular on the old houses of Nejd and goes back to ancient Babylon, reproduces precisely the pattern of the palm trunk when the branches have been neatly trimmed.

The date palm has flourished and multiplied. From the very large numbers in Saudi Arabia today (estimated at 6–7 million trees) one might imagine that it was the easiest tree on earth to cultivate, but in fact this is far from the truth. It is a complicated tree whose propagation requires skill and knowledge. For one thing, palms are either masculine or feminine; only the feminine trees will bear fruit and then only if they have been pollinated with flowers from a male tree. As the flowers of each are almost identical in appearance the cultivator must know what he is doing at this stage.

Trees can be grown very easily from date stones (anyone who has tried gardening in Arabia will have tired of pulling up the seedlings), but male and female palms come up in equal numbers although one male to every hundred females suffices. The sex of trees grown from stones cannot be determined for several years, therefore the cultivator prefers to grow his trees from offshoots which sprout from the stems of young palms, and which will grow true to the parent plant. These offshoots must be encouraged to root and need careful handling during transplanting. The females will begin to produce fruit after five or six years; they will bear between 25 and 100 kilos of dates per year and can live to be one hundred years old.

Despite the inevitable presence of numerous date groves among and around the houses of all the oases, each one has a very distinctive character of its own. This is their charm, and provides a great part of the pleasure of travelling around Saudi Arabia. No two oases are in any way the same.

Khaybar, some 160 kilometres north of Medina and 200 kilometres south-east of Al Ula, is one of the strangest oases of all. It is set in the heart of a great bleak lava-covered plain: a depressing place to travel, where the solidified lava stands clearly on the sands on which it came to rest. In gaps among the black rocks the candelabra-shaped daum palm raises its curving branches, its useless fruit as unproductive as the land in which it lives.

Khaybar is as black as the land in which it is built: the houses are of basalt, the valley cliffs behind them are covered with basalt too. Even the inhabitants are dark, for in the past the bedouin who owned the oasis found they could not live there because of the prevalent malaria and left the cultivation to their slaves. The village is built on the slopes of a valley at the base of which are extensive palm gardens. In summer and early autumn the bedouin camp on the slopes above, and come in to collect their share of the date crop. A little market, selling fruit and meat and household goods, has developed beside the palm gardens.

The oasis was not visited by a non-Muslim until the Italian traveller, Carlo Guarmani, came there in search of horses in 1864. He found the village consisted of seven districts, with some 2500 inhabitants. When Doughty visited the oasis a dozen years later the

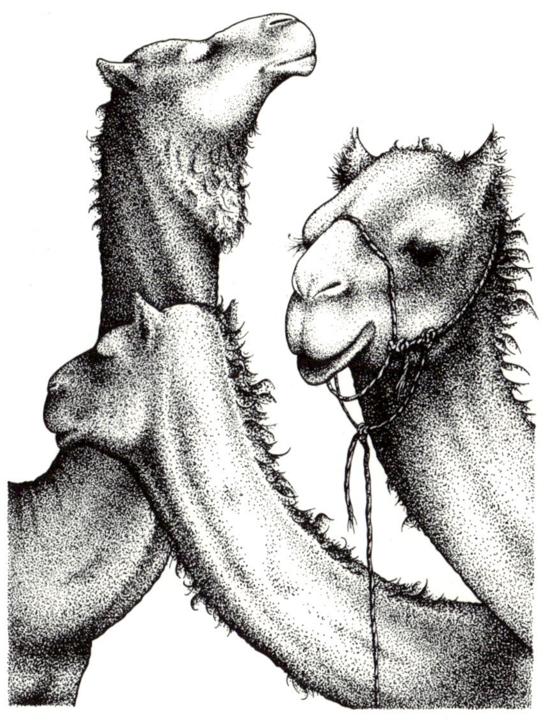

CAMEL HEADS

inhabitants were so shocked to find a Christian among them that he was held a virtual prisoner there, awaiting a ruling from Medina. Even as late as 1950 St John Philby found the oasis 'preserved almost intact by its natural defences against the motor car'.

Things could hardly be more different today. The main highway from Jordan to Jeddah and Mecca runs through the high street of the town. Heavy lorries pull up continually at the petrol station, and fair-haired foreigners shop at ease in the little market, their requests interpreted when need be by the school children eager to practise their newly acquired command of English. Khaybar is now firmly on the map.

So, indeed, is Tayma, some 255 kilometres further north. It lies on the same asphalt highway as Khaybar, in a hollow among almost equally forbidding terrain. All around is particularly arid, desolate grey-white desert, featureless and characterless. Driving across it for hour after hour one has the frightening feeling that one will never arrive – then suddenly, there is the welcome sight of the tops of palm trees ahead. The road sweeps down into the town, cutting through a high mound at right angles to its path. This mound marks the sand-drifted remains of an ancient city wall, which runs for some 3 kilometres around the whole oasis town, and still rises about 10 metres high. From the style of its construction archaeologists think the wall may originally have been built around 1200 BC.

The recorded history of Tayma goes back further into antiquity than that of perhaps any other oasis in Saudi Arabia. Due to a weird episode in the sixth century BC, the oasis became for a while effectively the capital of Babylon. King Nabonidus, who came to the throne of Babylon in 556 BC, started his reign in the traditional style of a Mesopotamian monarch, campaigning aggressively into his neighbours' domains. An inscription of his, found in the Harran, records: 'I took myself off from Babylon my city and took the road to Tayma, Dedanu (Al Ula), Padakku, Hibra (Khaybar?), Yadihu, and as far as Yatribu (Medina) where for ten years I moved among them and did not enter my city Babylon.'

In fact Nabonidus spent his ten years in Tayma. Perhaps the very remoteness of the place appealed to him, for he was having religious disputes with the people back home. Tayma was a town he could hold and he set about developing it and building palaces there. The ruins of Qasr ar Radim may be the remains of his palace. He lived well, too, having food and delicacies brought across the desert from Babylon, as the cuneiform records relate: 'He brought back from Tayma and sold the camel which carried the King's food to Tayma,' says one, and another mentions fifty shekels of silver paid to a camel man sent to Tayma with flour.

Finally Nabonidus was obliged to return to Babylon which was under threat from the Persians and was soon to fall to them. His Arabian 'holiday' was ended and the oasis declined after his departure. Until recent times Tayma remained a remote 'oasis apart' so that when St John Philby visited it in 1950 he could name the half-dozen westerners who had been there before him. The oasis had been held in semi-independence since 1916 by Ibn Rumman, who had liquidated the Turkish governor and all his bodyguards and built himself a strong mud fortress with an iron door. He went further to assure his own security by razing the eastern and western suburbs of the town to give a clear view of any approaching enemy.

In 1950 Ibn Rumman was assassinated in his turn by a cousin who was then promptly killed by his victim's bodyguard. At that point King Abd al Aziz sent troops to the oasis which was peacefully

OLD WATER WELL

incorporated into his realm. Philby, as a result, was able to visit the area without trouble, and was shown the recent graves, lying side by side, of Ibn Rumman and his assassin.

Recent years have brought rapid development to the oasis, comparable only with that undertaken by King Nabonidus himself. The great well of Haddaj, ancient heart of the oasis which was worked since antiquity by as many as seventy camels at a time, is now effortlessly drawn by diesel pumps. The main street, still a sand-covered little road when I first drove through four years ago, is now a dual carriageway with high standard lamps and pavements; asphalt has been run along the shady side lanes and there is a paved children's playground and schools for boys and girls. Three petrol stations supply the endless stream of vehicles which must fill up here before the long desert haul to north and south. Among the palm trees pomegranates, grapes, peaches and lemons flourish thanks to the sweet water flowing endlessly from the great well.

A rival perhaps in antiquity and certainly in fertility is the oasis of Jauf, some 350 kilometres north-east of Tayma and currently being linked to it by a new asphalt road cutting across the northern tip of the great red Nefud desert. Jauf, whose ancient name of Dumat al Jandal (mentioned in the Book of Genesis) has now been brought into use again, is one of the most charming and original oases in the whole kingdom. The name Jauf means 'depression' and is well chosen, for the old town is sited on the slopes of a great basin floored by a white salt pan and enclosed on three sides by steep cliffs. On the fourth side stands the new town and alongside it the ruins of the old, stone-built town. Above them towers the great Qasr Mared, perched precariously on a precipitous rock from which its walls have clearly slipped here and there over the ages. It has been patched and repatched since it was first erected, possibly in the third century BC, and today its keep stands in tattered tongues of stone.

Near to the castle is a pretty stone-built mosque also of venerable origin. It is believed to have been founded by the Caliph Umar in the early years of Islam and hence is among the oldest mosques in the land. It stands intact today, among the ruins of the old city, and mats are still spread in its prayer hall between the twenty-seven squat, square stone pillars. The minaret is particularly beautiful, of dry-stone work curving gently to the top. The pathway runs under an arch right through the minaret which is supported by huge stone rafters above. Three windows on each side pierce the tower, which is like no other I have seen. 'Why don't you climb up it for a better view?' an aged inhabitant suggested to us, but we did not like to do so and were content to admire from below.

Beyond the crumbling stone walls of the old town, and the white concrete buildings of the new, stretch the palm groves, orchards, and even meadows of the oasis. In these fields full of grazing cows, surrounded by high banks of reeds, more than anywhere else in the kingdom, one might wonder to oneself, 'Is this really Saudi Arabia?' Dumat al Jandal, sheltered in its great bowl, seems to belong to a green world of its own. It is protected from the red dunes of the Nefud which stretch away to the horizon, but in fact was always a prey to marauders – from the Assyrians who raided Adumn, as they called it, in the early seventh century BC, to Nabonidus of course, and so on to the late nineteenth century when Lady Anne Blunt described it as 'battered by wars'. Only in the present era of peace has Jauf been spared the sieges for which its fortress was built and is now no longer needed.

AN OLD HOUSE IN QATIF

More green still, yet somehow less unexpected in their desert setting, are the vast palm grove oases of the Eastern Province, Qatif and Al Hasa. Here the date palms grow to an extraordinary height, their tall elegant stems soaring above the dense undergrowth of fruit bushes, reeds, even grass, and vegetable plantations. Here must be the true home of the date palm, as told in the Sumerian legend. Despite the arid desert around them, these huge plantations seem so firmly established, so confident of their existence among the sands. And well they might, for this is the one area of Arabia where sweet water wells to the surface unaided in a series of powerful springs. Here the undergrowth can grow as lushly as it likes, for no one will shut off the pumps when a given corner has had its ration of water. The great underground water table bubbles to the surface here and is led off in a maze of little brown streams, the haunt of fishes, frogs and cicadas, and – in Hasa – large concrete-lined canals. The oases extend for many kilometres in all directions; their palm groves are cut through by wide alleys with the air of bridleways. They are a perfect green haven for the people of the towns of Dammam and Qatif which border the Qatif oasis, and Hofuf at the heart of the Al Hasa oasis.

The latter can enjoy yet another natural phenomenon among their palm groves: the cool caves of the Jebal Qarra. These golden

THE ENTRANCE TO THE CAVES IN HOFUF

sandstone hills have been eroded and sculpted to produce fissures and tunnels running into the heart of the mountain where even in the burning heat of midsummer a perfect dim coolness is maintained. The region's strange beauty is to be enhanced by development as a large public park.

11
The Quest for Water

Perhaps the strangest of the kingdom's oases, from the point of view of its water supply at least, is that of Al Kharj. Al Kharj is in fact so large that it might be considered rather as an 'agricultural area' than as a classic oasis. It is different, too, from the other extensive oases of the Eastern Province, Hasa and Quatif, in that it does not consist of miles of palm groves but quite simply of arable farm land. Its fields are stocked with grain and vegetables and shaded by high hedges of tamarisk trees; here and there is a chicken or dairy farm with a herd of cows of European origin.

At the heart of this farming area is the little town of Al Kharj, some 80 kilometres south of Riyadh. The town itself is sheltered in part by palm groves, it is true, but climb any hill there and you look out over miles of farmland rather than waving palm fronds. The non-desert atmosphere is enhanced by the delightful green park on the south-east side of the town, where families come to picnic in shady alleys, on lawns or among flower beds at the weekends.

What can be the source of such abundance in the heart of the desert? one might wonder. In the case of Al Kharj the answer is clear to see. Some 6 kilometres west of the town centre, near the brow of a hill, the rock surface of the ground has collapsed in two places and fallen into huge deep pits. Far down in these pits, which are some 100 metres in diameter and perhaps 130 metres deep, is clear, sparkling sweet water. It is the underground water table, the source of water for so many of the kingdom's oases, which is here exposed to view. Diesel pumps work day and night to raise the water from one of the pits, while abandoned pumps and water wheels stand on the lip of the other, in which the water level has dropped sharply due to pumping over the past ten years. A substantial canal leads away from the active pit, carrying the water out into the network of irrigation channels which feed the miles of crops.

At one other spot, nearer to Riyadh, the deep underground water table can be seen. This is in the even more dramatic pit of Ain Hit, 35 kilometres out of Riyadh along the Al Kharj road, and under the foot of a high cliff to the east of the road. Here the ground has fallen away and a great arch of rock spans a gash at the cliff foot into which which one can climb, descending in increasing gloom for what seems a very great distance. At the bottom of the immense pit a clear sweet-water river runs; birds perch in the arching rock dome above and swoop down to the water.

Water was pumped from this pit also, in the past, and an abandoned little pump house stands out in front of the escarpment, a landmark for those seeking to visit the pit. Today however the pit is not used; it is visited only by the curious and those eager for a swim in its cool shadowy depths. Twice during this century, however, the pit has played a role in the kingdom's development. One winter night in 1902 it was visited by a group of camel riders coming out of the desert, who watered their camels there before making a desperate attack on the strongly walled town of Riyadh. The leader of the group was the young prince, Abd al Aziz ibn Saud.

Years later, at the request of this same young man, now King Abd al Aziz ibn Saud, a group of American geologists were prospecting for water in the Riyadh district, during the gloomy years when oil failed to spurt around Dammam. They visited Ain Hit where, it is recounted, they were delighted to recognize rock structures of a kind which convinced them that oil must be found in the kingdom. They returned to Dammam to work with renewed hope and the following year were rewarded with the first great oil strike.

Just as oil was formed in ancient times and became trapped in vast underground reservoirs, so too the water which we see today in the pits of Al Kharj and Ain Hit is of extremely ancient origin. It fell in Arabia in the distant past, when the world was wetter and the deserts of today supported grasslands and forests. Fossil wood and ancient rock carvings of animals which require a more temperate clime, are evidence of the dramatic changes which have occurred over the millennia in the climate of Arabia. Today's exiguous rainfall of about 6–8 centimetres a year is no longer sufficient to stock up the great underground reservoirs and where they are exploited the water table is generally falling. Under much of the desert of Saudi Arabia, however, a sweet-water table can be found, provided wells are drilled deeply enough to reach it.

Riyadh is the city which, above all, depends on these ancient water supplies. This inland desert city, the largest in Saudi Arabia and with a population which is rising rapidly towards the million mark, is so far from the sea that it has not up to now appeared an attractive proposition to supply her needs with desalinated sea water. The alternative has, indeed, been ready to hand, far below the rock ridge on which Riyadh is built. In the past her inhabitants had found that they could reach sweet water simply by sinking deep wells under their town; these old wells are in fact some of the deepest used water wells in the world.

In recent years geologists have been exploring the larger ancient aquifers which lie under the desert to west and east of the city, and which contain vast reservoirs of water which may be 30,000 years old or more. Largest of these are the Minjur aquifer to the west of the town, from which water is already drawn in large quantities, and the Wasia aquifer to the east of the town which is now being developed.

The water, which is drawn up from great depths (the Upper Minjur for example is 1200 to 1500 metres below ground) is distinctly hot – too hot, in fact, to be useful, so it must be cooled from around 52°C to 30°C before it can be distributed through the city's water network. It also tends to contain a higher proportion of salts than is acceptable and much of the geological water drawn from below ground needs to be treated to reduce the solids content. As the city's population soars, industry is developed, and gardens and parks spread around the town, the need for water is escalating. In 1975 Riyadh was using some 130,000 cubic metres of water per day; by 1981 it is expected to need around 530,000 cubic metres. A desert city's water supply is the one thing above all others which cannot afford to fail. The geologists are convinced that the reserves of water in the deep aquifers are so great that they will not be depleted in the foreseeable future.

The discovery and exploitation of these deep water resources requires all the skills of modern technology. 'We determined the depths of the Minjur aquifer by geo-electric surveys and seismic refraction methods,' a hydrologist recalled. 'Radio-isotope dating showed us that the water in the Wasia aquifer was probably substantially recharged during the last pluvials, but in one well the water was shown by this method to be modern, seepage we suppose from the run off above the Wasia.'

Men have always had to work hard for water in Arabia and in centuries past, before such sophisticated methods of water exploration were available, sheer manpower linked to careful observation were their main resources. In the early centuries of Islam, especially, massive civil works were undertaken to control and exploit such water as was available from the country's scant rainfall. Most impressive of these works, perhaps, are the large series of ancient dams in the Taif and Khaybar districts, several of which have been dated to the first century of Islam. 'Those dams were amazingly over-designed,' a modern engineer commented. Apparently in their efforts to ensure that their structures would survive, the ancient dam builders undertook far more labour than was necessary. Their dams are often as wide at the base as they are high (like the Thalbah dam west of Taif which is 10 metres thick at the base, 10 metres high, and 8 metres wide at the crest). Unfortunately this labour was often wasted for the dams (including that at Thalbah) were not cut down into bedrock and were frequently breached by the flood.

In their early years, however, they held considerable reserves of water; the storage capacity of several of the Taif dams has been calculated at 500,000 cubic metres of water, while that of Sadd Qusaybah, south of Khaybar, must have been many times greater. The dams must all have suffered from the intractable problem of rapid silting however. 'They must have silted up in two generations as far as I can see,' a civil engineer remarked. His opinion certainly seems to be borne out, if not for the time factor then at least for the end result, by the state of several of the intact dams today; these look more like overgrown terrace walls than true dams, with the ground level up to their very crests on the upstream side.

Clearest example of this silting is the notable Sadd Saisid, north-east of Taif. Here the silt laps right over the crest of the 68-metre-long dam, which is nevertheless estimated to have had a storage capacity of 500,000 cubic metres in the past. The silt terraces above the dam can, of course, still be cultivated although its original purpose is now lost.

The other major dam of the Taif complex which is still intact, Sadd Samallagi to the south of the town, is considerably more impressive to look at than Sadd Saisid, for it is still relatively free-standing. It is about 190 metres long, 10 metres wide at the crest, and 10 metres high above ground level; it must originally have appeared higher for the ground level has certainly risen on both sides, due to silting. This dam also has inscriptions, mostly prayers, from the first century of Islam.

Some of the dams of the Taif region were connected with extensive channels and irrigation works which carried the water a considerable distance from the reservoirs. The problem of carrying water for any great distance was always one which taxed the engineers of ancient Arabia, for water in shallow channels exposed to the sun would rapidly evaporate. A widespread solution to this problem was the construction of qanats, underground water chanenls which sometimes ran for many miles, and from which the water

MOONLIGHT OVER THE DESERT

would not be lost. Access to these qanats (for repairs etc.) was assured by a series of chimneys at frequent intervals along the water course. From above ground one sees only the tops of round wide chimneys, marking the line of the water course. A qanat of this kind crosses the main Mecca–Taif road below the escarpment; it was first constructed at the orders of Queen Zubaydah (around 800 AD) to provide the city of Mecca with a reliable water supply.

Today's water engineering in Saudi Arabia is not confined simply to methods made recently available by modern technology. Time-honoured methods of water conservation and exploitation, such as the construction of wells and modern dams, also play an important role. Dams are of particular value since rainfall in the kingdom tends to occur in short heavy bursts, causing flash floods which run off down the wadis destroying all in their path, only to sink unproductively into the sand at the end of their flow.

Numerous dams have been constructed during the past decade, of which the largest is that in the Wadi Jizan in the south west. This big dam is some 40 metres thick at the base and reaches a height of 35 metres. It contains a reservoir with a capacity of nearly 19 billion gallons (about 75 million cubic metres) and will irrigate an area of over 300 square kilometres. Another major dam was recently completed in the mountains above, at Abha, to provide water resources for the town, while forty-five smaller dams have been built in the wadis such as those near Taif and Hail; an ancient dam near Khaybar has also been completely renovated.

New deep, government-constructed wells, worked with motor pumps, are now providing water throughout much of the desert for the nomadic bedouin population and their flocks, who are thus no longer dependent on the kingdom's unreliable rainfall. Similar wells, sunk in the more fertile wadis, help to supply the needs of many of the kingdom's towns and cities, and indeed are widely used throughout the land. Many of these towns are growing at such a great pace, however, that normal wells – in however promising positions – can barely meet their needs. Jeddah for instance has been supplied with drinking water from the springs in Wadi Fatima since 1947, and from those in Wadi Khulays for nearly as long. But the city's needs have soared and today she is taking some 18 million gallons per day from the wadis and agriculture is suffering in consequence. The city, however, is already estimated to need 40 million gallons a day and this quantity is increasing yearly. The wadi wells clearly will not suffice.

Surprisingly perhaps, the solution was found nearly three-quarters of a century ago, though no one at that time could have seen just where it would lead. In 1907 a strange new machine was imported to Jeddah from England. It became known as the *kindassa* (an Arab version of 'condenser') and was in fact an early distillation machine. The authorities had seen that the only source of sufficient water for the large number of pilgrims, who spent a month or more each year in Jeddah, was the Red Sea, and that if the Red Sea were to become drinkable the salt must first be extracted from its waters.

The condenser worked reasonably well for twenty years, fired by imported coal (which did not always arrive in time) and during times of trouble by scrap wood which did the machine no good at all. Finally it succumbed and in 1928 King Abd al Aziz imported two new machines, which eased the city's water situation until Wadi Fatima water became available.

Today the kingdom has opted without reserve for the modern equivalent of the *kindassa*, desalination. 'Of course desalination is expensive,' an official admitted, 'but in Saudi Arabia we have really no choice. We must rely on desalination to meet our needs. By combining electricity production with desalination we can keep the costs down to an acceptable level. And in any case, all water in Saudi Arabia is expensive.' Indeed, Saudi Arabia must be the one country in the world where petrol can be cheaper than water.

Small desalination plants were brought into operation between 1969 and 1975 at Jeddah, Al Wajh, Dhuba, Khobar, Khafji and Umm Lujj. Today plants are under construction or already completed at practically every town along the Red Sea and the Arabian Gulf shores. The kingdom has opted to make the massive investment necessary for the project now, while financial resources are readily available, so that in the future the water needs of her population will be assured. By the 1980s Saudi Arabia will be the world's largest producer of desalinated water, with an output of over 400 million gallons per day.

The largest plants are naturally sited at the main urban centres and are being constructed in stages so that a phased production is assured from the start. Al Khobar, Jeddah, and Medina are destined to have the highest production, mainly for civilian consumption. Rivalling the desalination plants for these city complexes are those which are to be built for the two giant industrial complexes of Yanbu and Jubail, where the water needed for the petro-chemical complexes and the townships which will develop around them will be provided by desalination. Rapidly constructed desalination plants were indeed among the first priorities for these sites.

The initial phases of the larger desalination plants are already producing electricity – 50 megawatts per day from Jeddah Phase I, 100 megawatts from Jeddah Phase 2 for instance. They make a useful contribution to the city consumption, but this is small by comparison with the many hundreds of megawatts a day which will be produced in the later phases of these and other plants.

With the rapid development which has taken place over the past few years, Saudi Arabia has found that man's first need is still for water, and that city dwellers consume far more than desert people.

12
Minerals in the Ancient Rocks

The third great quest which has occupied the Saudi authorities in recent years, after the search for oil and for water, has been the search for minerals. While oil has been the real bonanza, the possibility of developing other mineral resources is also a genuinely interesting one. No country likes to see all its eggs in one basket, for one thing, and on the other hand successful industrialization calls for mineral deposits on the home front.

The Directorate General for Mineral Resources, which was set up in Jeddah in 1961 to undertake exploration of the country's minerals, is currently moving into an elegant new headquarters building a little inland of the Hamra Palace. The DGMR has been assisted since the start by two of the world's leading mineralogical organizations, the US Geological Survey and the French Bureau de Recherches Géologiques et Minières. In 1976 these two organizations were joined by a third, Riofinex, a subsidiary of Rio Tinto Zinc.

From the point of view of mineral resources nature distributed her favours in Saudi Arabia with a remarkably even hand. Roughly speaking oil, the greatest of all resources, is found in the east; other minerals are found in the west, and hence the Jeddah base for the DGMR. The sharp differences in the structure of the land which harbours the various resources is perhaps more clearly visible in Saudi Arabia than in any other country, making the search for minerals something in which even the layman can find a real interest.

The western region of the country is a dramatic landscape of mountains, valleys, and the cliff-like escarpment of the southern Hejaz and the Asir. It is a beautiful region of changing colours, the rocks showing clearly the layers of which they are made. Around Medina, for instance, a ridge of harder rock protrudes from the tops of the hills, like the crest along the back of a dragon or a dinosaur. On the escarpment road between Mecca and Taif stripes of pink and grey rock alternate in the cuttings, showing at their most dramatic in a striped pinnacle isolated by the road building. Veins of coloured marble or white quartz shine from the hillsides, unencumbered by vegetation.

When we first drove south along the main road from Tabuk we were enchanted by the changing colours of the landscape. Naïvely we hoped at every turn that Jeddah would be set in scenery like that before us; we were totally surprised and somewhat disappointed when we finally came suddenly on the flat, hot coastal plain, the only variety being provided by mirages which danced in front of us and made us constantly expect to see the Red Sea before our eyes.

The Red Sea itself is perhaps the most dramatic evidence of the great disturbances which have shaken western Arabia throughout the millennia and which are, incidentally, the source of her mineral wealth. In the ancient past one could have walked across from Arabia to Africa for the great trough, which forms the Rift Valley of Africa, the Red Sea and on north to the Dead Sea and the Jordan Valley, had not then opened. Some 30 million years ago, however, the continents split apart and the Red Sea was formed. A glance at the map is sufficient to show how the two coastlines of the Red Sea should fit together, but it seems unlikely that they will do so again, for in fact they are still drifting apart at a rate of some 2 centimetres per year.

Inland from the sea the pressures of movement caused folding and faulting which threw up the high mountains of the Hejaz and the 'land of Midian' to the north of it. The mountains were further shaken, throughout the ages, by periods of volcanic action which have left their picturesque traces among the hills and valleys here. This is, in fact, one of the most extensive areas of volcanic activity in the world.

Looking down on the Hejaz from an aeroplane it seems as though here and there some giant hand had overturned a bottle of ink. The black fluid has run down the hillsides and along the neighbouring valleys leaving an indelible spider-shaped stain. Driving down the road from Tabuk, the impact of the ancient volcanism is even more impressive: in the region of Khaybar abrupt cliffs of broken black-brown boulders stand petrified on the yellow sand. Behind them is a sterile sea of dark, depressing basalt; before them the warm colours of the living desert.

These dead volcanoes begin to exert a fascination. What was the source of such vast lava flows, one wonders; whence did they come and why did some break up into great blocks while others set in swirls and coils like pools of over-thick oil? One looks out for cinder cones, the smooth conical hills built up entirely of volcanic ash and cinders, or for the horseshoe-shaped remains of once-active volcanoes. Several districts are particularly interesting to explore in this respect: one lies in the south between Khamys Mushayt and Dhahran al Janub, where great cinder cones and ash layers are clearly visible from the main road; another lies between Taif and Medina, well away from the asphalt roads.

Medina itself is no stranger to volcanic activity: it was, indeed, the last district to be hit by an active volcano, and the only one of which an historic record exists. In the thirteenth century the inhabitants of the city were suddenly aware of the earth trembling, and of a strange noise to the east of them. A great lava flow appeared and flowed red-hot towards their city. At night the sky was so bright from the fire of the volcano that people could see to sew while sitting on their roofs. They prayed urgently that their city be spared, and so it was; the lava flow halted just short of the sacred city and her people were saved.

From a little to the east of Medina, near the village of Hanakiya, a track runs south towards Taif, passing between vast areas of *harra* (lava flows). Somewhat to the east of this track, and about 250 kilometres north-east of Taif, is one of the most exciting volcanic regions of all. It centres around the small village of Al Hofr (which means 'the pit') and is itself sited between two ancient cinder cones. Across the wide plain here a number of cinder cones are scattered, while 6 kilometres north-west of the village a clear horseshoe-shaped cone and another broken one mark the site of a vast crater (which presumably gave the village its name) and which is the largest volcanic crater in the western region. We had some difficulty finding the place for the bedouin really could not believe that we were seeking a big hole. Will they tell their children of crazy westerners driving through their deserts looking for holes in the ground?

The crater, which is called Waba, is huge indeed, some 2 kilometres across and 260 metres deep. It is thought to have been formed by a great explosion deep underground which threw out a mass of earth, rock and volcanic debris, and in doing so cut right through an older volcano at its lip. Today a huge salt flat sparkles white in the base of the crater, and palm trees are cultivated on a ledge part way down the cliff, thanks to water which oozes through the near-vertical sides of the crater at that point.

Sweeping around the northern side of the crater is a dense black lava flow whose swirls and coils are as clear set as if they had poured across the ground only yesterday. The lava flow ends abruptly, in a cliff about 3 metres high; the upper surface of the flow continued a little further than its base and has broken off, here and there, in great slices. This lava flow is clearly relatively recent, and newer than the crater around whose lip it flowed. The crater itself is newer than the two volcanoes beside it, and is thought to be only a few million years old, quite possibly less.

Volcanic activity in the western region goes back some 30 million years, however, and among this old volcanic terrain are found some of the rich deposits of minerals for which the western region has long been known. When the modern geological survey teams began their exploration of the western region the first thing which caught their attention was the signs of extensive mining for metals in ancient times. The best known of all these ancient mines is in a volcanic area of great antiquity, only 100 kilometres north of the Waba crater. The mine is known as Mahd adh Dhahab ('The Cradle of Gold'), and was no new discovery to the geological teams, for it had in fact been worked in modern times, from 1939 to 1954, as well as by ancient miners.

Mahd adh Dhahab is all that one could desire of an ancient mining site. Huge ancient grinding stones, piles of old slag and others of smooth, multi-coloured rock cylinders from modern drilling, litter the area. A great hill of weathered lava has been sliced across in a series of trenches of terrifying depth. These trenches followed veins of quartz in which gold, silver and copper were found. They were painfully excavated in the early centuries of Islam, and at an earlier period still, perhaps around 1000 BC, by lighting fires on the rock, then pouring water onto the heated rock to make it crack. Working in this way, in the confined space of the deep narrow trenches and the great heat of the Hejaz, must have required an effort which only great rewards could have made worth while. In the 1940s and early 1950s the Saudi Arabian Mining Syndicate, which reworked the mine, extracted 766,000 ounces of gold and 1 million ounces of silver. Did the ancient miners, who after all were the first-comers, do even better? Today the mine is being worked once again by the British company of Consolidated Goldfields which found promising signs of gold at the foot of the hill in 1977.

At a neighbouring ancient copper mine known as Umm ad Damar, a team of French geologists were drilling when I visited the district. They had made themselves comfortable in an air-conditioned tent (was this a sign of the future for Saudi Arabia's bedouin population?) and succeeded in offering our unexpected party of twenty a three-course meal in traditional French style, despite the incredible remoteness of their desert camp. At Umm ad Damar vast pits with collapsed tunnels leading off them mark the ancient workings. Huge piles of shiny brown-black slag show where the rock was smelted to extract the ore. The slag, which covers a large area, is estimated to amount to some 100,000 tons. Large quantities of early Islamic pottery lie among the piles, showing that this mine, like Madh adh Dhahab, was worked in the Middle Ages (Mahd adh Dhahab pottery and inscriptions have been dated to between 700 and 1100 AD).

Here too there seemed to have been earlier, less-well-fired slag, below the glassy smooth Islamic debris, indicating much more primitive and presumably far older mining efforts. Why, one wonders, were these mines worked energetically for centuries, and then abandoned for centuries after? One theory is that their working may have coincided with damper periods in the peninsula when there would have been adequate quantities of acacia wood available for the fires needed to smelt the metal. In dry periods, perhaps, the trees would have died and charcoal for the fires would no longer have been obtainable.

Hundreds of these ancient mines lie from north to south throughout the western region, and as far east as Dawadimi on the road from Taif to Riyadh. Many lie near the great caravan routes of the Hejaz and the Darb Zubaydah. Attempts to date the lower levels of charcoal have given, in some cases, dates as ancient as 1000 BC, which coincides with the early use of the great spice routes. Possibly metals were carried from here along with the spices by the passing caravans.

Today mineral exploration has gone far beyond the immediate neighbourhood of the old mines, for modern methods can detect ores which the ancient miners could not find, and modern needs have increased the range of minerals required. The whole Arabian Shield is being mapped geologically, and the search has extended beyond this area to the north and east. Exploitation of finds already made is only just starting, but Sheikh Zaki Yamani has said that he expects that the kingdom will become one of the world's major exporters of minerals in the next twenty years.

Apart from gold, silver and copper, the main targets of the ancient miners, nickel, zinc and lead have been found. Interesting deposits of phosphates have been discovered in the extreme north west, and it is hoped that they may one day match the important Jordanian phosphate deposits in the same region. Iron ore deposits, estimated at 350 million tonnes, have also been found in the extreme north west and the British Steel Corporation is evaluating their potential. Also in the north deposits of uranium have been found. In the south west there are huge deposits of table salt, which in the

Jizan dome alone are estimated at over 33 million tonnes. In the bottom of the Red Sea itself mineral-rich brines are now being investigated and assessed.

While these are the major minerals discovered to date, signs of many others have been discovered in the ancient rocks of Arabia. Their exploitation, however, cannot always be immediate and simple. While the ancient mines lay on what were then the main trade routes of the Middle East, these routes look to us today no better than sandy tracks, unsuited to the kind of transport which would be needed to evacuate the minerals recovered. Many of the modern discoveries have been made in regions where there was not even an ancient track.

Road building is, however, progressing at such a pace throughout the kingdom that each year more regions come within economical reach of an asphalt road and the prospects of exploiting newly found deposits become more interesting. Saudi Arabia is doing its best to encourage foreign mining companies to work in the kingdom, with a five-year tax holiday, guaranteed repatriation of capital and profits, and a clearly worded mining code. Local industries are already being established which are counting on making use of the kingdom's own mineral resources in the near future. A fertilizer plant planned in the extreme north west, which would use the phosphate deposits of the region, is an example of this.

Forty years ago no one would ever have tipped Saudi Arabia as a leading oil exporter. Today who can foresee which of the kingdom's other natural resources will make world headlines in the future? In the past her gold mine of Mahd adh Dhahab was the greatest in the whole of the Middle East and Africa; Saudis are optimistic that some of today's discoveries might lead to mines of international status in the future.

13
Era of Prosperity

The era of prosperity which has dawned in Saudi Arabia in the present decade is certainly merited insofar as those who have known total deprivation deserve their share of the good things of this world. Of all lands, those of the Arabian desert have perhaps been consistently the poorest throughout the centuries. Only very briefly in the past, and in certain districts, was a little luxury known: the Nabataeans prospered and left elegant stone-cut tombs at Medain Salih; beautiful Hellenistic bronzes were traded at Fau on the edge of the Empty Quarter; in the early centuries of Islam fine things were imported from the Arab Empire – the litter of fragments of delicate early Islamic glassware at the ancient port of Jarr near Medina is a relic of this trade. But by and large the Arabs of Arabia have known only hardship throughout their lives.

'The summer I passed thus fasting and bedouin-wise, lying upon the elbow', wondering 'with the hollow thought "What shall be for this day's life",' wrote Charles Doughty, who spent a year or more with the bedouin just a century ago. He lived as one of them, eating the food they ate and with no other resources. As the year wore on he grew weaker, and by the end of the summer could scarcely ride his almost equally weak old camel. The picture he paints, of a people lying all day in the shade of their tents, not moving lest they provoke a thirst they could not quench or a hunger which they had no means of satisfying, haunts the memory as more typical of the bedouin's lot than the heroic tales of war and raiding.

Arabia's poverty had one positive consequence. When the Turkish empire fell and the European states rapidly extended their influence across the Arab lands, no one was tempted to move into Arabia – no one felt that the nascent Saudi state or its rivals were urgently in need of tutelage or protection. The Arabs of Arabia were left, by and large, to run their own affairs.

Their deprived past continued, in fact, almost into the present.

Although oil was found in the 1930s it could not be substantially exploited until after the Second World War; the income it brought in then was far from huge and the state was only saved from a balance of payments crisis in 1958 by the timely accession to the throne of Prince Faisal. Faisal ruled as a cautious and competent King; a measure of his country's future prosperity only became visible shortly before his death early in 1975.

Now, when almost everyone in the West knows someone who has visited Saudi Arabia or worked there, it seems strange to recall that a decade ago the reaction to a remark about Jeddah was likely to be: 'Jeddah, where's that?' Today Saudi Arabia's leading cities are firmly on the world map; it is surprising how much people abroad know of the kingdom's geography and leading personalities, rather than how little.

The transformation is due to a single substance – oil. Oil was known in the past of course: in ancient Mesopotamia and Dilmun it was used to caulk boats and to make waterproof pots. A seepage near Mecca was blocked in 1880 by the Sherif who feared it might attract unbelievers. However, its great value was only appreciated in this century and Saudi Arabia was not one of the forerunners in the oil race. Today, however, she is out in front. Even when oil production is limited to 8.5 million barrels per day the kingdom enjoys an annual income of some $38 billion. Even with the current wide-ranging development plan which aims to bring the whole country up to modern standards, the income from only 6 million barrels per day would suffice. Saudi Arabia can in fact produce more, and is now boosting her production capacity for the future. There is virtually no limit to the income which the country could allow itself, were it to choose to exploit its resources rapidly. With her relatively small indigenous population (the official estimate of 6.5 million includes 1 or 2 million foreigners), these oil revenues give Saudi Arabia one of the highest *per capita* incomes in the world.

How best to spend this money for the good of the state and her people has been one of the major concerns of the ruling family, the Al Saud, and their ministers and advisers. For the first fifty years of its existence, the Saudi state was ruled by its great founder, King Abd al Aziz ibn Saud, whose major preoccupations were to create national unity and security within his realm. Until late in his life he had to work for these aims with no great wealth to back his endeavours; his success stemmed from the strength of his own personality, from his comprehension of the desert people and from the wisdom of his judgements.

His successors, King Saud, King Faisal and King Khalid,

have been chosen from among his older sons, who are supported by numerous brothers, sons, nephews and cousins. The ablest of the royal princes are given an advanced education in the United States. Many of them serve as ministers and officials, and in key positions in the armed forces. King Abd al Aziz's policy of choosing wives from all sectors of the population has created a large and strong royal family with widespread contacts. Their government is strengthened by the collaboration of other ministers, drawn from the population as a whole, usually technocrats with a PhD from an American university. These ministers and senior government officials come from many walks of life which include not only the leading merchant families, but men of relatively humble origin as well. Ability rather than family has been the criterion in their appointment.

In recent years it has been necessary to decide how to spend the increasing oil revenues to provide the facilities that were lacking. Twenty-five years ago there were hardly any paved roads in the kingdom; Saudi boys and girls who wanted an education were sent to Egypt, or possibly to English boarding schools; medical care of any substance was available in two or three towns only; much of the country was unmapped, relatively unexplored.

Limitless wealth does not, unfortunately, make development effortlessly easy. An example is education. 'Of course we can build the schools, providing we can bring in sufficient construction materials, produce accommodation for the builders, and decide on suitable architectural plans,' one official remarks. 'But then we have to find teachers, often by choosing suitably qualified people from abroad, and textbooks which fit our needs and do not conflict with our religious beliefs or political views. You see that the provision of even one primary school, let alone a secondary school, is a major achievement.'

Thus development problems escalate. In a country which, until recently, produced next to nothing, most raw materials must be imported. To do this, sufficient road, port and airport facilities must be constructed and these require more raw materials, both for the actual construction and in the provision of accommodation for the construction workers. Since modern education has only recently been widely available, there are insufficient qualified Saudis to take charge of all these undertakings, or even to decide who should take charge. So skilled foreigners are imported in large numbers; choosing these foreigners, and organizing their housing, schooling, food and other needs places further strains on the system. Finally, in a land where the population is small and lacks modern skills, even the construction workers must be imported, housed, fed, provided with water and electricity and transport. To Saudis it sometimes seems that a disproportionate amount of their resources is being devoted to the foreigners; for Saudi planners there is the concern that the foreigners should not exert a disproportionate influence, nor disrupt the traditional patterns of Saudi society by the example of their alien lifestyle.

Despite these great problems and constraints, the kingdom has made astonishing progress in the past few years. The road network has spread with amazing speed in what one seasoned foreign consultant described as 'the greatest road building programme since Roman times'. Twenty-five years ago there were 237 kilometres of paved roads, mostly in the oil areas of the Eastern Province; by 1970 there were 8,434 kilometres and by 1978 an estimated 16,000 kilometres in a still rapidly expanding network.

School building has rivalled that of the roads, with an equivalent of one new school opened every day of the year in 1977. The numbers of students of all levels have now topped the million mark; about 100,000 of these are adults catching up on past lack of opportunities by attending literacy classes today. Since all education is segregated, small towns must be provided with a duplicate series of schools if girls are to be given equal educational opportunities. At present nearly three times as many boys as girls attend school and it is they who will provide the educated work force of the immediate future since relatively few of the girls are currently able to work.

Housing and hospitals, water supplies, drains and electricity, as well as the massive industrial undertakings of the gas-gathering project and the petro-chemical complexes of Jubail and Yanbu, are other priorities for state spending. Here also the effort involved is great. The present target of providing electricity for every village may sound simple until one remembers that villages may be hundreds of kilometres apart, and as far again from a paved road. They are few and far between, in fact, and spread over an area the size of Europe.

There is no doubt that the people are pleased with what is being done for them. 'It is good to live here today' is a frequent comment. 'Our great country' is another common expression. Saudis are genuinely happy to be Saudis and not a few foreigners would like to acquire that desirable nationality, now reserved almost exclusively for the native-born. While wealth has undoubtedly spread throughout the population, and schooling, subsidized school meals, motor vehicles, transistor radios and television sets are within the reach of most (apart from geographic constraints), the effects of the present spending power are most clearly seen among the emergent middle classes.

Saudis spend their new wealth much as westerners do, on domestic equipment and a better home, holidays abroad and finally a second house in Europe. 'We are hoping that the manor house will soon be sold. Some Saudis arrived yesterday by helicopter to look over it', remarks a villager in the depths of the English countryside. Particulars of top-level London properties are now produced in Arabic and even country estate agents have learnt to look to Arabia for buyers of their best properties. The writing, one might say, is on the wall – in Arabic. It is the Saudi equivalent of the English yearning for a holiday cottage in the Dordogne, but written large like everything else in Arabia.

The ease of foreign travel is an important factor of life in Saudi Arabia today. Even the bedouin, and villagers from the most remote oases, appear to feel quite at home travelling by plane. For the city dweller a holiday abroad widens the horizons, and offers a break from the hectic pace of development at home. Saudis can find all they require for their leisure time in London or Paris, just six hours away. They have no need to foist western patterns of relaxation on a society at home which they feel is not ready for such things. Indeed many Saudis are adamant that they would not wish to see such developments in Saudi Arabia, that the kingdom's role should continue to be that of defender of Islamic values.

There has of course been social change and an important aspect of this has been the establishment of the principle that 'a Saudi's home is his castle'. There he can live and entertain as he chooses without fear that, for example, his gramophone records will be seized as they might have been thirty years ago had he played them too loudly. Today, on the contrary, well-to-do Saudi homes are stocked with the latest in record and cassette players, tape recorders, radios and television sets.

Such possessions are particularly prized by Saudis who still feel somewhat diffident about pictures, sculptures and books. The large villas of the middle classes are also expensively furnished, often centrally air conditioned, and equipped with the most elegant and modern of bathroom fittings. In a land where water has always been in short supply, opulent bathrooms are now rated one of the greatest luxuries.

Saudi wealth is now being enjoyed by many other than the Saudis themselves. The kingdom has become the modern El Dorado, with foreign workers flocking to make their own fortunes. There are now thought to be around 2 million such workers; the second Development Plan alone envisaged bringing in half a million skilled foreigners. If they stay and complete their contracts, and can resist the temptation of a spending spree on their home leave, most foreigners can save enough to buy themselves a house back home after two or three years working in the desert. But they can expect to work hard, often living in prefabricated camps, in total deserts and with no leisure pursuits. Many of the Korean road builders, for instance, are out on the site from dawn to dusk, and opt to work on Fridays too, not only for the overtime pay but also because there is nothing else to do.

Even those foreigners who live more comfortably, accompanied by their own families in an apartment or villa in the cities, find that they are expected to work hard for their money. Their Saudi employers pay well but expect good service for the generous salaries they offer. Most foreign workers will also be employed on a fairly short-term contract. A few companies, such as Aramco and the Saudia airline, keep their personnel for a lifetime, but most expect them to go home once their specific job is completed. A few foreigners do move on to another job once their own is finished; virtually none can stay for ever, however. Saudi nationality is very difficult to obtain and of course available only to a Muslim.

Along with the rise in the number of foreigners visiting or coming to live in Saudi Arabia the kingdom saw an even more dramatic rise in her influence in the international field during the 1970s. In the short space of three or four years, Saudi Arabia became one of the leading powers in the Middle East, one of the most influential of Muslim states. Such a role might seem a difficult one for men with little experience at the international negotiating table, who are themselves younger in general than their foreign counterparts, and first-generation graduates. Yet the old bedouin tradition of democratic leadership, of rule by consent, and of courteous persuasion has stood them in good stead. The Saudis have not given the impression of parvenus in the world councils; they have negotiated with the skill and confidence of oldtimers.

The Saudis have enjoyed from the start the benefit of clear-cut policies of whose value they are convinced. Their major aim in the world has been to further the interests of Islam, and to this cause much of their foreign aid has been devoted. It has involved them too as champions of the Arab cause in the conflict against Israel, and they have also naturally adopted a leading role in the struggle against communism. This has brought them firmly, if at times somewhat uncomfortably, into the western camp where they urge a more active role on the West in combating communism. While Saudis see their primary role as leader and supporter of the Arab and then the Muslim states, they are also very ready to act as a bulwark against the spread of communism in the Middle East and Africa.

In the use of her great oil power, Saudi Arabia is anxious not to weaken the western democracies, since that must be to the advantage of communism. Hence hers has been the restraining voice in the councils of OPEC; and so great are her reserves that her voice has prevailed.Her new wealth has brought greater stability to the peninsula, a stability which it is her aim to maintain, while building up the peace and prosperity of the region around her.